LOST

FOUND & REWIRED

Lost, Found and Rewired:
Mind Tools to Shift You from Stressed and Frazzled to Calm and Vital

Cover design by Ida Fia Sveningsson Konsult
www.idafiasveningsoon.se

Book layout by Logotecture
www.logotecture.com
ISBN: 978-0-9983277-3-0

writeStream
PUBLISHING

Writestream Publishing, LLC
www.writestreampublishing.com

LOST

FOUND & REWIRED

Mind Tools
to Shift You from
Stressed and Frazzled to
Calm and Vital

Cynthia Dougherty, Ph.D.

CONTENTS

FREE GIFT

As a way of saying thank-you to my readers, I have a very special gift for you! My eBook, *10 Must-Have Mind Tools for Frazzled Women*, can be downloaded by going to my website:

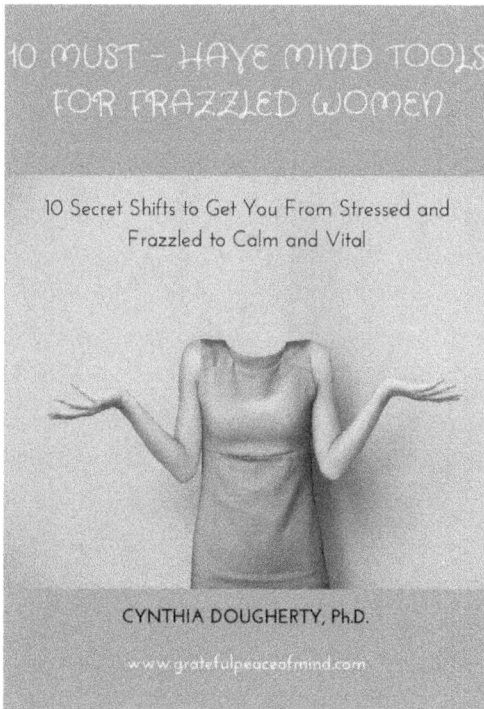

http://gratefulpeaceofmind.com/free-gifts/

FOREWORD

Let me share a little bit about Cynthia Dougherty. She is an oxymoron. At first glance, you might say she's a blonde bombshell and make assumptions based on that. As the saying goes, never judge a book by its cover...because beyond that flowing long blonde hair, stiletto heels and beautiful face is a person with a brilliant scientific mind, a Ph.D., and a background in Neuro-Psychology, who is wise, insightful, and has a heart that overflows with love, compassion, spirituality, and kindness.

Because of her extensive studies and real-life applications of her knowledge, she uses "mind tools" to shift her thinking to gain greater peace, clarity, and happiness. From a painful divorce to even more extreme situations, Cynthia was able to use her mind tools to shift her thoughts and emotions, quickly, from hysteria and fear, to calm and action, as her entire home was being engulfed by flames. These are the precious tools that Cynthia shares with all of us in this book.

I am grateful to Cynthia for wanting to share *LOST, FOUND, and REWIRED* with the world.

If you have a mind that wanders to the negative more often than not, this book is for you. If you are exhausted from constant worry, fear, and stress, this book is for you, too. If you can't seem to be still and shut off that distracting mind chatter...this book is definitely for you. And for those who already live a mindful life with meditation, this book will bring added value to your practice.

This book is a gift. It is a deliciously empowering, at times humorous, practical, and open-hearted guide that will literally help you turn your life around. Lost, Found & Rewired helps you break patterns of negative thinking and gives you easy tools to shift you from worry, sadness, and fear, to gratitude, peace, and happiness, no matter the external situation.

I am honored to write this "Foreword" for Cynthia...because in the true essence of the word, this book will give you the tools you need to move your life "forward" ...in a more joyful, mindful, playful and peaceful way.

Blessings and Love.

By Patricia San Pedro (aka Positively Pat)

Four-time Emmy Award-winning TV producer, communications executive, twice-published author, photographer, breast cancer survivor/advocate, and inspirational speaker.

"Dish & Tell" co-author - Published by Harper-Collins 2005

"The Cancer Dancer" author – Published by San Pedro Publishing 2010

www.PositivelyPat.com: Health and wellness community

Link of Hope Sistas is a support group under Positively Pat. We help, empower, and give hope to women around the world as they travel their own cancer healing journey.

"Joy is the Choice"

TO MORGAN AND SHELBY

"Act on your guidance without constantly saying that you are frightened and require proof that you will be safe. You will never get that proof. Every choice in life is an act of faith. Stop letting fear be the one constant voice you listen to with unremitting faith. Be outrageously bold in your belief that you will be guided but do not have expectations of how that guidance will unfold. Keep your attention in present time always in present time...." ~Caroline Myss

"The Work always leaves you with less of a story.
Who would you be without your story?
You never know until you inquire.
There is no story that is you or that leads to you.
Every story leads away from you.
Turn it around; undo it.
You are what exists before all stories.
You are what remains when the story is understood."

~ Byron Katie

INTRODUCTION

MINDING YOUR BRAIN CHATTER TO CREATE A PEACEFUL,

HAPPY LIFE

I used to wake up and question my very being.

I wondered if I was losing my mind. I felt so stressed that I just wanted to pull the covers over my head and pray for a blizzard.

The endless daily issues being thrown at me, with no end in sight, were exhausting me.

I know I'm not alone in feeling this way. If you feel this way too I understand.

Several years ago, I faced great adversity. I had to negotiate my way through the most challenging decisions of my life. I was not looking for balance: I was struggling to survive. In the depths of my despair, I pulled myself together through mindfulness and rewired my thinking. In fact, I rewired my brain.

This book is both the story of my personal journey and a guidebook about how you, too, can use these techniques and methods.

My background and training is as a Neuro-Psychologist. I had my own practice for many years. You may wonder, *"How does a person with a background in neuro-psychology find herself with such dilemmas?"*

Looking back on that turbulent time, I see the answers clearly. When I was in the middle of it, however, I was blind to the huge red flags that insistently waved their warnings right in front of my face. I lived with intense fears and anxiety. I burdened myself with extraneous preoccupations. Like many human beings, I let my emotional responses

– guilt, anger, loneliness, helplessness – intensify my pain. My education and training did not stop me from suffering.

WHAT REALLY LED TO MY DOWNFALL?

It's simple, really: my unwise thinking patterns.

Rather than view my losses as a clearing of a new path to the future of healing and well-being, I allowed negative thoughts to consume me until I believed I was in a black hole with no options of ever climbing out. I spent my days anticipating an uncertain future, regretting the past, and never living in my present. In my heightened state of stress, it was incomprehensible to me that all would be well because the universal fear of the unknown guided my path – with no clarity to be found.

Back then, I simply couldn't see that I was repeating the same life patterns over and over again in my relationships and my thoughts.

I hope by reading my story, I can help you reach a fuller understanding of how we all tend to get in our own ways. By the time you finish, you will learn how to rewire your brain by understanding the importance of *mindfulness* (minding your chatter) in the creation of a productive, peaceful, and happy life.

Just by changing the way you think, not allowing your mind to control you, and giving your brain a rest twice a day, you can transform your entire life. It really is that simple.

BUT HOW CAN I BE SURE?

Let me share with you my personal story.

On November 10, 2001, I made a terrible decision that sent my whole life into a tailspin. At the time, I had just emerged from a painful divorce from my high school sweetheart. I was in the middle of a career transition. I was moving from working as a school psychologist to the corporate world, teaching companies to integrate psychology into their policies. My marriage ended, and I suddenly found myself the single mother of two children. I had lost friends on September 11th, and I was grieving.

My life, as I'd known it, was totally upside down. Intellectually, I knew that this was not the best time for decision making. But I craved change. I worked with a woman who owned a consulting firm. She was a brilliant professional with multiple degrees, who had written a book that focused on hiring psychologists as corporate consultants. I learned a great deal from her; mostly that I wanted to integrate my educational experience within large companies. She spurred my career change.

At this same time, I also felt a craving for greater spirituality. I met a woman named Vanessa who introduced me to meditation. Vanessa also works as a psychic and medium. She told me that I would meet a man who would "rock my world." I would know this man because he would wink at me during a social event. I was so taken in by her conviction of my future, and so fearful of entering into another commitment that at parties I stared at people's shoes for what felt like a lifetime.

What I never did was stop and consider whether 'rocking my world' was a good thing. In 2000, I attended a Christmas event. I'd just returned from a business trip to Europe. I was jet lagged, and let my guard down while standing in line for a glass of wine at the party. When a handsome man without socks addressed me, I looked up to respond, and he winked at me. My first response? Panic. That initial reaction was the first of many signs I chose to ignore, and so "rock my world" he did.

I had lived a sheltered life, and "Wink" represented everything unfamiliar. I was a woman who had married her best friend her sophomore year in college. My life was about education, working, and raising children. This charming, well-travelled entrepreneur had no children and an appetite for adventure. He was also athletic, fun, social, and romantic. He had an admirable ability to mix and mingle in any crowd.

We were obviously different people. Vanessa warned me that he would be a 'free spirit' and nothing like a 9-5 man. I was skeptical at first and waited six months before I went out with him. The first night I stayed at his house, a woman came banging on his front door the next morning. Wink went outside to talk to her, presumably so I couldn't hear the conversation. However, I heard her accuse him of using her. But I was infatuated. I ignored what my instincts were telling me – I even ignored the fact that Vanessa, who was arguably responsible for my attraction to him in the first place, didn't like him at all. He was charming. I was charmed.

Geography was another challenge to our relationship, as we lived a few hours away. But, my initial skepticism about the possibility of a fulfilling relationship soon crumbled. I was overwhelmed by my life. He appeared to be my knight in shining armor, ready and willing to make it all better.

Now I know I didn't need a knight in shining armor. What I needed was a brave friend to question my sanity! However, since mindfulness was a foreign language to me while I remained firmly fixated on the future, who's to say that I would have even listened to a friend?

After six months of dating, Wink and I became business partners. I put my house in Maryland on the market in preparation for our move to San Diego. In the beginning, everything seemed to be going my way. I had six offers in the first four hours the house was on the market! However, one problem after another prevented the deals from closing. This *should* have caused me to take a step back and contemplate whether it was a sign from the universe that I should stay put. Unfortunately, it had the opposite effect and intensified my desire to get out of Dodge and avoid confronting my unfinished past.

So, I packed up two dogs, two cars, two kids, and went on a long cross-country ride. I was fortunate to have my friend Gail join us. She started out as my nanny and became family. To this day I consider her my 'mother.' Her husband had recently passed, and she was up for an adventure. And what an adventure it was!

On my first night in town, exhausted, and staying temporarily in a hotel, we went to a little place called "Bully's" to have a quick bite. It had been a stressful trip. I had recently learned that due to my ex-husband's tax problems, there were too many liens on our house to settle it easily. The trip consisted of many stops to call lawyers and fax documents. I was tired. I was disappointed in my ex for caring so little about our children's future. So I wasn't in the most perceptive place of mind, and I completely missed it when I received the biggest warning of all when I met a cowboy sitting outside of Bully's, wearing a cowboy hat and boots, along with shiny, turquoise jewelry.

Hello? There are no cowboys in San Diego. DING DING DING!

With no introduction, he walked up to me and asked where I was from. I guess I looked like I was new in town. He told me to move back home with these sobering words:

Lady, these people around here are fakes. They are out for themselves and cheat on their wives. Everyone looks the same. You have no idea who has money and who is broke. You look honest; be careful. I am giving you fair warning to move along.

My immediate reaction was that he must have had too much to drink. I never saw him again, and no one I spoke to had ever heard of him.

My life in California was a far cry from the happy ending I desired. On the contrary, it was challenging, frustrating and painful, partly because I had no clue about the reality of being an entrepreneur. Entrepreneurship is nothing short of a rollercoaster ride for risk-takers with strong stomachs. For a family, it becomes a feast-or-famine lifestyle characterized by instability.

I lived for the future. I was never in the present. Therefore, I was constantly anxious and fearful. Worse, when I smiled and pretended all was well, I became invisible and lost my entire self. When times were bad, I isolated myself from friends and family. When times were good, we shared with others and enjoyed the relief. No matter what, I put everyone else first and me last.

I'm sure you can relate to putting everyone else first and yourself last.

I could not comprehend how to focus on *me* without feeling guilty. I became a shell of my formerly confident, successful, and well-respected self.

It's impossible to count the number of red flags, intuitive impulses, and advice from concerned family and friends I ignored as I pushed against the raging rapids in my persistence to make this work, somehow, some way. I'd take two steps forward then four steps back as events conspired to get my attention.

Our house burned in a fire. I'll tell you more details about this story later, but you can only imagine how traumatic this was.

I suffered the loss of many family members, including my beloved father. My father and I were always close, but he didn't like that I moved across the country with Wink. He didn't trust Wink – hello? Another waving red flag I ignored – and I missed him terribly after we left. He had a quadruple bypass right before we left, and his health declined from there. He moved from nursing home to nursing home. Although I was with him when he died, it broke my heart to have left him. I often thought about moving back, but I wanted my children to be able to graduate from their schools in order to maintain stability.

We moved into our dream house, only to lose it to foreclosure in the end. I had no idea that we were financially so badly off and so in debt. Rentals were hard to find, and the sellers' market was good. Whenever we found a nice place, the landlords wouldn't renew the lease because they found a buyer.

These were tremendously stressful and traumatic events. However, through it all, I kept my sanity and remained positive, determined to inspire those around me to find the silver lining and the lesson in every hardship. Material things are just that and can always be replaced. I tried to focus on that, feeling grateful to be alive.

When you see a river of fire surrounding your entire neighborhood, there is no time to think about what you are losing. You count your blessings. You are happy to be uninjured and your family intact. The same applies to the destruction of your house. At the time, it feels like the worst (and scariest) experience you could ever endure. However, if you keep pushing against the flow of life, it will eventually push back equally hard until you learn the lesson.

In January of 2012, I made the painful decision to take a leave of absence from California. Both of my kids were attending college in LA, my relationship was in disrepair, and nothing seemed to be working in any aspect of my life. The economy was terrible, and we could not find jobs. There were days when we only had one meal to eat. My husband's family refused to allow us to move to Philadelphia with them, and my family would only take me back in Maryland without Wink. They hated him, a secret I kept from all of our friends. It was a difficult decision, but the constant stress was taking its toll on my health. I couldn't eat and was down to 92 pounds. I packed two suitcases and flew to the East Coast.

During my first two months, I grieved.

My life as I knew it was over. I was separated from all of the people and things I loved the most. I lived in fear of uncertainty for so long, I could not let myself go and just relax. Instead, I obsessed over issues beyond my control.

How Meditation Saved Me

It's amazing how distancing yourself from your life and taking time for meditation can add a dimension you never knew was there.

We live in a chaotic, information-abundant world of social media, multi-tasking, immediate gratification, and noise. There is lots and lots of stimulation everywhere we look.

Where does stillness and quiet fit in? How does stillness and quiet fit in?

I took the opportunity to welcome this time in my life as a gift instead of a travesty. That revelation did not occur overnight. It took weeks of stillness. I began to see parts of my life that were toxic and questionable as I journaled many thoughts and unanswered questions. I reconnected with friends and family. I re-engaged in society and rediscovered things that made me feel happy.

My Life Was About To Take Another Major Change

During this process of being still, I reached out to a person I knew in San Diego who had moved to Miami. I'd socialized with "Carlos" and his wife several times and thought of them as a fun couple. Carlos seemed to be a man of great integrity. He was a Cuban immigrant and a self-made man. He had friendships that dated back for decades. Initially, I thought I could pick his brain about career options. In our conversation, he revealed he and his wife were no longer together, and, eventually, we began to date.

He was intelligent, funny, strong, and confident. We enjoyed each other's company. He loved to take road trips. We could ride in the car for hours, carrying on conversations without skipping a beat. He lived in Miami, and we would regularly fly back and forth to see each other. Much to my delight, he was also looking for a partner with whom he could share his life.

I moved to Miami to be with him. My kids transferred to local colleges in Miami. I took this as a sign that life was transitioning smoothly. A few years later, we married. As I looked for opportunities to keep my identity without losing myself in a relationship, I began to write again. That process led to an invitation to write a chapter about mindfulness for a book on breast cancer[1]. At the same time, I became involved with wellness and life coaching. I also started a certification program for teaching meditation.

As I traveled through the stages of inner peace and stillness, cracks in my relationship with Carlos began to surface. My normal was not his normal. I felt like I needed a stronger voice and presence in our life and home. Everything around me was his. Although I was grateful to be a part of his life, and I enjoyed his company, I wanted our home to be a reflection of both of us. I wanted to paint some of the rooms and buy new bedroom furniture.

He was generous to many friends, family members, and charities. He had many fine qualities. But he was resistant to change, and incorporating me into his life was a change he could not manage. He wanted a stress-free life and had very specific ideas about what that meant. He wanted to travel to certain places at certain times. He wanted to go to restaurants – the same restaurants on the same nights – rather than having dinner at home. He watched his television shows, and not what I wanted to watch. He kept track of every penny that came in and went out and required that I give him every receipt for every purchase. After my past financial disasters, I saw this as a benefit rather than a manner of control.

I often felt as if I didn't belong in his life. He liked his old familiar bedroom furniture – I did not like sleeping in a bed other women had slept in. He made it clear that I belonged in his life and was a great part of it, but my children and extended family were not a part of the 'package.' He wasn't mean to them – he helped with their education and they lived with us. It's just that he wanted my undivided attention. And so, I wanted to spend time with him alone, as a couple. I wanted to go away with him during the summer to regroup and build better communication. I wanted to focus on the things that drew us together instead of the things pushing us apart. Instead, nine months after an amazing and joyous wedding, he decided not to join me, and he asked me for a divorce.

---

1 "Miami Breast Cancer Experts" by Cindy Papale-Hammontree and Sabrina Hernandez-Cano (2015).

What, Then, Is The Lesson?

What I did not understand at the time was that I was going through a purification process. Just as a forest is cleaned by burning the underbrush, I needed this painful fire to make my roots, my mind and body, healthier.

When upsetting events transpire in your life, it is important to sit back and look for repeating patterns in your thoughts and behaviors. I set about reflecting on my life, while at the same time moving forward. I cocooned myself in a small eastern shore town, locking myself away in the stillness of water, ducks, and mindfulness. I continued to work on my meditation certification while I kept writing. Writing helped me process these very confusing life events and gave me some distance to observe the patterns in my life. The more I learned about meditation and mindfulness, the more I realized how much it jived with what I knew about the brain from my years as a Neuropsychologist. It all made sense.

After I completed my training, I celebrated at "Theo's," a local spot where pear martinis are like liquid gold. While sitting there sipping my martini, I began talking to a wonderful woman named Kathy Fong. The energy between us was undeniable. We were sisters from another mother. We had an intense spiritual connection. Kathy and I shared a passion for spreading the word of mindfulness and meditation. Finally, a sign that appealed to my heart, mind, and instinct. I learned the power of my own abilities from my relationship with Kathy and learned what I really wanted to do – teach others to rewire their brains and find peace and happiness and strength, the same way I had.

And so, after nearly fifteen years of chaos and heartbreak, I finally found peace. I thought I had lost my mind – but it turns out I just wasn't looking in the right place for it. I was too busy focusing on the wrong things to mind my mental chatter. When you find yourself, like a phoenix, rising from the ashes – in my case both literally and figuratively – you want to share the story of your transformation with others. You don't have to be a Neuropsychologist or certified in Meditation training in order to Rewire your brain in the ways you need to make this work for you.

CHAPTER ONE

MEET YOUR BRAIN

"Every time you take in the good, you build a little bit of neural structure. Doing this a few times a day – for months and even years – will gradually change your brain, and how you feel and act, in far reaching ways."
~ Rick Hanson, "Buddha's Brain: The Practical Neuroscience of Happiness, Love, and Wisdom."

If we genuinely desire a less stressed, more creative, and happier life, we need to understand a few facts about our behavior and our brain. Neuroscience is my passion in life, and it can be explained in terms that don't require a PhD to understand. I believe that once you understand how your brain is wired, things will begin to make more sense to you. And, when you understand how it *is* wired, you can understand how to *rewire* it.

Let's Begin with Neuroscience

Neuroscience is a fast-growing subject of interest these days. It's a broad term that describes the field of study that helps us to better understand our brain and how it impacts our behavior and cognitive functions.

The brain is constantly changing. Everything we do in our daily life changes our brain. Our experience allows us to focus on these brain nerve cells from their beginning and how they grow and connect. We have over 100 billion nerve cells – how cool is that? These cells contribute to our motivation, sadness, memory, and critical thinking, among other things.

The journey of life can feel like a constant climb over endless challenges. Have you ever noticed that even when your life feels balanced and stable, you can still feel apprehensive? Even if you don't know why they exist, these feelings of insecurity can derail happy moments. We question our worthiness while we wait for the other shoe to drop. When we are happy, we can't just leave well enough alone. We must find something to worry about or stress over.

Think about this scenario: You are having the best day ever. Everything is going beyond your expectations. Your boss gave you a raise, and you found a twenty-dollar bill in your pants pocket. Do you stop and think about how grateful you are for such an amazing day? Or, like most people, do you start listing all of the reasons why it could never happen again, or how tomorrow's events could never come close to today's good fortune? Do you question whether you deserved a raise in the first place? Or maybe you feel guilty for having such great luck?

How about this: have you ever met a genuinely nice person, had a great conversation and information exchange, and then, instead of looking forward to another get-together, you question what could be wrong with this person? Because in your mind you keep telling yourself: *this guy is too good to be true.*

It doesn't make any sense, does it? Good things are happening, and we are waiting for the other shoe to drop. We are too busy worrying to enjoy the good things that have happened. Alternatively, we get what we want, and we feel deep in our hearts that it must not be real.

The good news is that this kind of thinking is not our fault. You see, it's in our DNA. During difficult and overwhelming times personally and collectively, it is human nature to question ourselves and our abilities to get through chaotic and painful times. Our brains are wired this way. Why is this? Why do we tend to always think the worst, even when so much positivity is right before us?

Believe it or not, when confronted with stressful events, it is often our mind that causes us the most difficulty. *WHY?* Because the mind immediately shifts to what is most familiar. Those prerecorded messages kick into gear as you remind yourself about your past trials and tribulations. As negative thoughts immediately flood our brain, right before our eyes, we see the worst possible outcome.

Our thoughts, feelings, and behaviors are all packaged together neurologically. They are based on amazingly complex sets of connections in your brain that can't always be predicted. Our mysterious brain creates millions of new networks every second. There is a lot going on in there! When we are sad, frustrated, or anxious, our minds habitually kick right into a negative mode. This is often followed by impulsive reactions that set us up for failure because what we think about, we bring about.

Throughout our life experiences, we typically develop a negative cycle of feelings, thoughts, and behaviors which result in negative consequences. These unwanted outcomes often reinforce a negative cycle, which means that over time we find ourselves repeating the same self-defeating spin on life, over and over again. When you look back at these events and truly examine your feelings, you will see patterns emerge. The feelings, thoughts, skills, and habits kick into overdrive and become an *automatic response* until the patterns and experiences become hardwired into our brains.

There is a good reason for all of this. Back in the cavemen days, the brain was developed to respond to multiple external threats and extraneous variables. While life appeared to be more simplistic way back when, the simple fact is that cavemen were faced with daily survival challenges, including having to run for their lives to avoid being eaten by a predator. They also confronted starvation, sickness, and conflicts between groups. It became self-preservation to expect the negative stimuli and be prepared to react to them quickly. We have carried this need to look for dangers, fears, and interpersonal problems into our daily lives. When the caveman brain is on alert, it can cause us to become fatigued, which reduces our immune system and leads to never-ending stress.

Think about your daily routine. While our lives today are much more complicated, our brains are still on high alert for threats. Every day, we're on the lookout for potential dangers, problems, and unpredictable situations. When we walk through a new situation, negative triggers divert our attention and help us decide whether to fight or run. You are trained to survive.

Do you ever wonder why some people are more positive than others? Or why other people never seem to be happy?

We all know at least one person that lives with a black cloud hanging over their head, always expecting doom and gloom. No one escapes adversity: grief, loss, and challenges are all part of everyone's life path. But how is it that some of us retain a positive outlook while others remain stuck and are unable to see beyond the darkness?

If you are in the latter group, let's take the pressure off because you are not alone. Everyone's brain is predisposed to negative thoughts and cycles. It is in our cells and our DNA.

As the most important organ in your body, your brain is involved in everything you do and everything you are, including your thoughts and feelings and your ability to get along with others and their behaviors. It's a heavy load for something that only compromises two percent of your total body weight! Your brain uses about twenty percent of your body's blood flow and consumes 20-30% of your daily calories. The human brain is made up of three main parts and is estimated to have been in existence in its present form for over 225 million years.

Think about this: Your brain has more connections than all of the stars in the universe and has the storage capacity for over three million hours of television.

In his book, "Hardwiring Happiness: The New Brain Science of Contentment, Calm, and Happiness,[2]" neuropsychologist Rick Hanson describes the brain as having a "negativity bias." We have a tendency to attract the bad and repel the good because the bad is always stronger than the good.

The intense upset that people experience when losing a bet with money, for example, tends to be stronger than the euphoria they feel when they win one[3]. An unfavorable recommendation about someone is more memorable than a good one. A bad mood is more likely to extend to the next day; however, a good mood will dissipate faster. If ten people compliment you, and one person criticizes you, which will you chew over the most in your mind? The praise or the insult?

Childhood traumas can last a lifetime. The brain evolved the 'negativity bias" mostly because negative experiences are more enduring. It helps us survive on a very basic level to remember the bad things and anticipate them and act accordingly. Unfortunately, this trait doesn't always translate well into modern life. As a result, we can recall all of the unsettling things that happened during our week, but can we name at least five good things? Can you name five tasks that you enjoyed at work this week? Can you list five traits you like about one of your coworkers? It's much easier to list five things you don't like. Early on, our brains are wired to compile lists of the negatives, which is why we notice undesirable behaviors much faster than positive ones.

Negative experiences, in contrast to positive ones, impact our survival significantly.[4] In essence, negative experiences are fast memory systems that convert into negative mental states, then into enduring negative neural traits. Once they become neural traits, they are effectively hardwired

---

2 Harmony Publishing 2013

3 This may have you asking the question – then why do people gamble, since they lose more than they win? The answer may be in where people find their pleasure. See the section on "the joy of the chase" in Chapter Two.

4 Roy F. Baumeister et al, "Bad is Stronger than Good." Review of General Psychology 5 (2001) 323-370.

into our brains, requiring rewiring to replace the traits that are harmful. Conversely, positive experiences, the source of our inner strength, take longer to transfer into long-term memory storage. Therefore, our positive experiences have a greater tendency to wash away before becoming hard wired while the negative ones stick like glue. We over-learn the negative and under learn the positive. Our brains are good at learning from the negative and bad at learning about the new, positive experiences.

Meet Your Brain

I want to explain the different parts of your brain so that you can understand the purpose of each part and why you react the way you do to certain situations and people. Understanding how your brain works may help you retrain it down the line. You can't fix what you don't understand.

Your brain is an integrated whole that works together with a symphony of the parts. Like the instruments in a symphony orchestra, each part has its own integral role that makes the whole thing function.

The first part of your brain I want you to meet is known as the amygdala.

The amygdala is shaped just like an almond. It is a part of the limbic system, the main source for your moods and feelings.

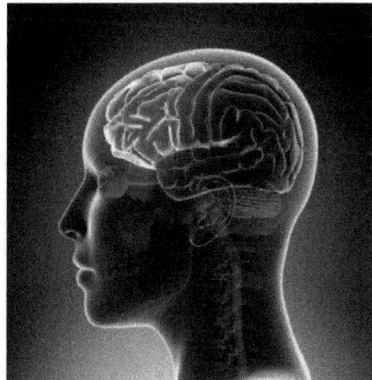

This almond is the guard of your being. Its job is to challenge each and every situation you encounter and tag it as either safe or dangerous. In this role, the amygdala constantly questions incoming situations. "Will this hurt me?" "Should I be fearful?" "Do I like this or hate this?" When something happens in your life, the amygdala starts to process the information, reacts to it, and then sends messages to the other parts of the brain. If our almond friend senses fear or danger, it sends a warning signal to the other parts – a message of crisis that prepares our body to either physically defend ourselves or get out and run. This is commonly known as the "fight or flight" response.

Your amygdala is used often every day. Whenever you are feeling threatened in any life situation, no matter how minor or major the threat, it kicks into gear. This could be your schedule, your job, your plans and goals, or your personal relationships. For example, if you go out on a date and another woman starts to flirt with your boyfriend, your amygdala definitely won't like that. When I was studying for the real estate exam as a way to make money in hard times, the amount of information seemed endless. It seemed overwhelming and impossible to remember all of the information. It was new, unfamiliar, and scary. I could barely breathe. It's critical to understand the rush you sometimes feel inside because the almond plays a huge role in our stress reactions.

Enter the Seahorse.

The hippocampus is named after the Latin term "seahorse" due to its shape. Although it serves many functions, for our purposes, it is also a part of the limbic system that regulates our emotional response. It is in charge of storing long-term memories and helps us to make them resistant to forgetfulness. In practical terms, this guy helps us remember where we parked our car at the mall!

The seahorse and almond work together in gathering information from our senses. If something is threatening, the alarmed almond sends an urgent message to the seahorse, which is the receiver of the hormones and transmitter systems serotonin, norepinephrine, and dopamine. This trigger, or "amygdala hijack," can raise our blood pressure and cortisol, making us feel panicked. This can cloud our judgment and increase our aggression, creating a snowball effect that makes everything worse instead of better. The partnership of the almond and the seahorse is important, as it keeps us alive. The almond senses the threat – the seahorse does something about it.

Remember, however, that we are wired for the negative bias. Consequently, we are always on the alert for possible threats. We often fear – and expect – the worst. Does this sound familiar? Your hypersensitive brain, combined with its natural tendency towards negativity, makes it difficult to lift yourself up and keep going. It is so much easier to tell yourself all of the reasons it's not worth getting out of bed this rainy Monday morning, rather than face the day with hope and optimism. Yes, you may have been on 100 disappointing dates, but this one might just be the one.

The cerebral cortex, the largest structure in our brain, is divided into four lobes.

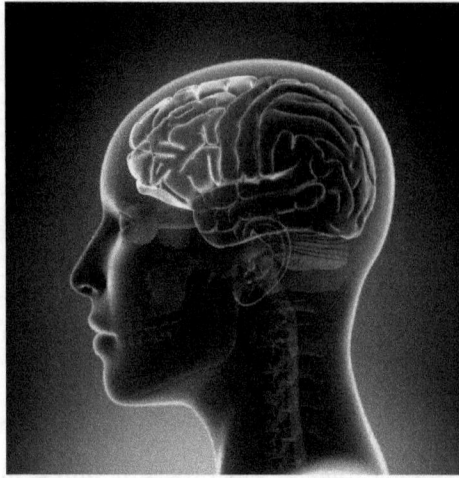

We'll limit our discussion to the frontal lobe, our next brain part of interest. Inside the frontal lobe is the prefrontal cortex. Sorry to say, there is no shape-inspired nickname here, so we'll just call it the PFC. The PFC makes up about 30 percent of the human brain. It is said to be the last to develop, often taking until our mid-twenties to be fully functional. Its function involves focus, attention, judgment, organization, planning, control, empathy, forethought, learning from mistakes, and impulse control. The PFC is the caretaker of the building: it helps us to decide, understand, inhibit, recall, and memorize. This region is a big deal. It's the only part of the brain that is connected to all of the other brain regions and functions. Pretty cool, if you ask me. As the CEO and orchestra leader of the brain, the PFC is the only part with a set of brakes.

What does that mean? Imagine why kids act as they do. It's because they're kids, right? Neurologically, what that means is that their PFCs aren't fully developed. An underdeveloped PFC is what we call 'immaturity.' The PFC helps us to stop feeling and thinking. It slows us down and controls our motor skills. It puts an end to fear and daydreaming and organizes the chaos in our lives. It is also responsible for our creativity and helps to adjust our emotions. This is all critical to our daily functioning in society. If someone has damage to their PFC, they have little or no ability to stop or inhibit their impulses. They just do whatever they want to do, because organically, their brakes have failed. They lack the ability to stop, think, and consider the consequences of their actions.

One more piece to the brain puzzle: Deep inside your frontal lobes lies the anterior cingulate gyrus. Since there is no fun name for this one, we are just going to call it the ACG.

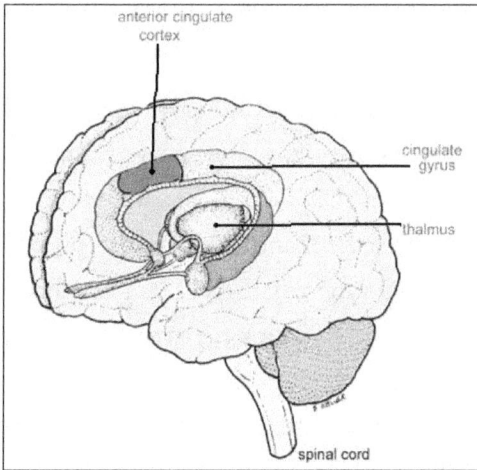

The ACG is responsible for detection and for shifting attention. It also regulates emotional learning, maternal instincts, motivation, goal-directed behavior, and autonomic and endocrine activities. The ACG can induce feelings of anxiety, pleasure, and fear. It causes changes to the heart and respiratory systems. This increases cortisol, the stress hormone, which can result in raise blood pressure and aggression. It is an area of vocalization for crying, laughing, and high-pitched sounds. I have an actual brain part responsible for my ugly crying or silly laugh – it's not my fault, it's my ACG!

Why is this important?

Neuroscience is much more popular these days than it ever has been because it gives us a better understanding of why we think and act the way we do. The business world is taking full advantage of neuroscience. Many of the marketing and sales techniques to which we are exposed daily are based on neuroscience research of the brain, which provides insights into our motivations for purchasing items, or for lingering longer in malls, restaurants, or casinos to spend more of our hard-earned cash.

We are born into a world that has a negative bias. We've discussed why our brains are wired to always be on guard, to expect the worst, and be prepared to either fight or run. This phenomenon keeps us in a defensive posture, where we're constantly on guard, less trusting, and self-focused. However, we can rewire our brains and make changes.

Cultivating a better understanding of why our natural responses to events in our everyday lives have a negative framework, and why those around us act and feel as they do is a crucial first step. How many people do you know that share the mantra, "Be prepared for the worst and hope for the best"? I know some days I feel like I am the only person I know who has a positive outlook. I look forward to the new day and the fresh experiences it will bring. And yet, there are days in which I fight the same urge as everyone else – to succumb to the self-defeating energy around me. It's built in. We all experience days when we question ourselves and think: *why bother?*

Consider a time when you felt scared or threatened. If you're like most people, you can probably think of many situations.

Let's review the brain structures we just outlined and illustrate how they function in real life situations. I'll pick an extreme one in my life: the night my house was on fire.

Throughout the day, we'd heard about a fire raging about an hour away from our house. It was one of those California forest fires that get out of control and begin to consume populated lands. We saw ash floating in the air. My gut told me this was not going to end well. But, neighbors consoled each other by saying that it was too far away to be concerned with. Still, I did not want anyone to go to sleep, so we stayed awake and close together. We all snuggled in bed and watched television until the power went out. Around 3:30 a.m. my daughter and I were walking down the stairs to get a drink of water when she looked out the window and saw flames at the back of our house.

For some reason, everyone always asks me what I took that night. I did not sit down to write out a list because, thankfully, my brain zoomed in and took control. I ran to the washing machine, grabbed my wet clothes, and put them into a pillowcase because I had this crazy idea that they might get mildewed if I left them too long. My husband remarked, "The house is burning down. There will not be a washer when we get back." That's when my almond kicked in and, like a charging lion reminded me of survival. My body needed a few seconds to go from the 'flight' stage to the 'don't panic and stay calm' stage.

The almond, together with my ACG, sounded a bell. The bell alerted my seahorse and my sympathetic nervous system to the PFC. Then, the almond alerted the control centers in my brain stem. My seahorse called out for cortisol, norepinephrine, adrenaline, and other stress hormones. My heart was racing, my mind and thoughts were speeding up, and I felt upset, rattled, and protective of all the living people and creatures in my house. Having never been in a fire, I was not prepared by experience for the loss of control of my mind, let alone the practical loss of electricity and telephone service. I was in the dark trying to find my cell phone and car keys.

Meanwhile, my almond was telling my seahorse to prioritize this experience for storage. By doing this, it was also telling new neurons to be forever fearful. To this day, when I smell smoke, my heart starts to pound. I sat on a step and told myself to take a deep breath. That one small step triggered my PFC to slow down, stop, and think. A few moments of stillness can make the biggest difference in our lives. Believe it or not, it saved mine. It allowed me to remain in responsive mode as opposed to the more frenetic reactive mode. I was in panic mode. Stopping to breathe and be still took me only a few moments, but it allowed my rational brain to take over and do what needed to be done in order to save myself, my family, and the few objects we needed to get through the next few days. I could think without emotion and stay centered. I reduced the amount of stress hormones in my body.

The example I gave you was obviously not an everyday situation. We can feel threats to our world at work or at home, and in much less dramatic ways than a house fire. Can you feel yourself being on the defensive when you are faced with a new or unfamiliar situation? Can you identify with pulling towards the negativity versus the positive and appreciative? Is your glass half empty or half full when you are faced with a situation in which you feel a lack of control? If your boss calls you into his office, or if you receive an unexpected letter from the IRS in your mailbox, the almond will kick in and make a snap judgment about the situation. Since the force of negativity is always stronger due to our caveman need to stay alive, our reactions to events like these tend to be fraught with anxiety. Most likely, your first thought wouldn't be, "I'm getting a raise!" or "I'm getting a refund!"

The negativity to which we have become accustomed automatically places self-blame with thoughts like, "I must be in trouble." This triggers our defense mechanisms and used to be a very useful survival skill. Since, in modern life, most triggers are not life threatening, the defense mechanism tends to be a little bit much for any given situation, and we need to learn to tone it down to fit the circumstance. We need to remember that our instinct is a normal pattern, but we can make positive changes by becoming more aware of our thinking, It will take some practice, but we can rewire our thought patterns.

CHAPTER TWO

LOOKING FOR HAPPINESS IN ALL THE WRONG PLACES

"So many conditions of happiness are available: more than enough for you to be happy right now. You don't have to run into the future in order to get more."
~Tich Nhat Hahn

What exactly is mindfulness?

Mindfulness is a simple practice that you can do anywhere. You can incorporate it into daily life to help break the cycle of anxiety, stress, unhappiness, and exhaustion. Mindfulness promotes happiness and peace and becomes more powerful the more you practice it. It becomes part of you and helps you deal with the stressful situations that life presents, with new courage and presence.

We will talk more about Mindfulness in general in Chapter 4, but here we will talk about Mindful Happiness.

Let me ask you a few questions:

- How do you define happiness?

- How often do you feel happy?

- Is your happiness contingent upon external events or circumstances or people?

A spiritual leader once told me to make a list of what makes me happy. Doing this activity inspired me to carefully consider the entire concept.

What would you write on your list? Go ahead and write it, if you think it will help. I'll wait.

The majority of my list involved making other people in my life happy. Spending time with my family, volunteering, traveling with my kids. All of that is nice, but once I looked at it I wondered, "Is this what is at the core of what makes me happy? Is my happiness all centered outside of myself?"

When I was first dating my ex-husband, I was overwhelmed one day when he told me that he lived for making me happy. *Wow!* I thought. *Who is this man?* No one had ever said anything like that to me before. His admission of this complete investment in my happiness created a deeper connection between us. It sounded wonderfully seductive, romantic, and intoxicating.

But in reality, are the people we surround ourselves with responsible for our happiness? Or is happiness more of an inside job?

If you're like most people, at one time or another, you've listened to a frustrated family member or friend complaining about a particular person in her life who wasn't making her happy. It's an easy trap to fall into: the 'you complete me' relationship. Meaning, "If I'm not happy it's your fault. I am not a whole being without someone else." There are so many people, it seems, who never appear happy. They are miserable 24/7 and rarely smile or express joy.

If happiness, then, is an inside job, its definition varies from person to person because we are all unique individuals. We may experience happiness as "a state of heightened positive emotion," "a state of well-being," or "a pleasurable experience." This positive emotion has a huge impact on our daily lives.

So, if happiness is a variable, what is Mindful Happiness?

Stop and think about it right now: at this present moment, are you happy?

Mindful Happiness involves the happiness you feel inside of yourself in this moment of time. *Period.* It does not include whether you were happy yesterday or even a half hour ago. It doesn't matter if you will be happy tomorrow or in twenty minutes. It has nothing to do with your predisposition to happiness. It is only the happiness that you feel *right now at this very second.* Stop and take a breath and tell me at this moment what in your life is bringing you a moment of happiness? For me, as I write this, I am looking over my computer and seeing the Chesapeake Bay. The soothing water makes me smile. Sometimes we are too quick to point out what is making us unhappy in the moment, with thoughts like, "How can I be happy when I am so stressed?" Or, "I can't be happy now because nothing is going right." But in any moment, there can be a sliver of happiness. You just have to look for it and focus on it.

Mindful Tickles: Finding the Joy in Little Things

I can sometimes find happiness with the small stuff with what I like to call "Mindful Tickles."

Here's an example of a Mindful Tickle: my dog Murphy is notorious for making me smile by flipping a toy over his head or sleeping with my shoe in his mouth. Other Mindful Tickles might occur when I take a minute to observe the entertaining people around me during lunch. At times, I crack myself up over the silly things I do inadvertently, like putting on a dress or a pair of Yoga pants and then finding out that they are on backwards. I'm sure you've had the experience of having so many crazy, unplanned events happen to you in a day that when the next one occurs, you just have to laugh. These are the brief moments of joy that put a smile on my face and make me laugh at myself, even on my most frazzled days. The trick is in noticing these Mindful Tickles amidst the sea of other stimuli that might not be as positive.

Sounds doable, right? Staying in your present, noticing Mindful Tickles, and being happy. But how can you be sure you are happy?

Let's face it: this is where the rub comes in with many of us.

The emotion of happiness is felt by each of us differently and is triggered by different things. What makes me happy may or may not make you happy. We did not enter the world with a one-size-fits-all happiness center in our brain. Our emotions, experiences and present mindset affect everything we do. Often, we have a terrible tendency to feel guilty or attach other negative feelings to being happy. Or, we put contingencies on our state of happiness: the "if...then" happiness approach. *If* it's a sunny day, *then* I will be happy. *If* I make more money, *then* I will be happy. *If* I get lots of gifts....*if* I find the right man...*if* I find the perfect outfit....The list of "ifs" can be endless. But there's a catch with this approach – you can't be complete and happy until your list of variables – things external to you – happen.

Thus, many of us get trapped into wishing for happiness in the future, based on the outcome of events and circumstances over which we have little or no control. It's the *happiness dream* syndrome. I know from my own experience how alluring and easy it is to be in a relationship with a person who puts their whole life on hold for the 'someday' or 'dream day' they believe is right around the corner, and encourages you to hold on. It turns into a dance you share as a couple that you are not even aware of. Just be patient – the lifestyle we want is coming! We are not happy now, but you wait and see – as soon as this deal comes through I will make you the happiest person in the world. I can't tell you how much of my life revolved around waiting to be happy someday. And when the deals fell through, or the promises were broken, my emotions took a sickening roller coaster ride.

Keep this in mind:

Standby happiness is not in any way Mindful Happiness.

My positive emotional state as I knew it was scheduled ahead of me in the weeks or months to come. I lived for my unknown but vaguely promised blissful future while I avoided the present. Worse, I convinced myself I was staying positive by planning my happy days ahead with the notion that I would receive something even bigger and better. I made vision boards of my happiness to come but missed the entire point of this exercise. I lived with a man who believed in '*anticipating joy*,' yet had no clue what that meant. Later, I realized that Wink lived for '*the joy of the chase*.' His mindful thrill and joy came from the potential of the reward. In all of my psychology classes, no one ever explained such a concept to me, but it is one sought after by many entrepreneurs and business people – and compulsive gamblers.

Neurologically, here is what was going on in our brains: As 'Wink' was receiving greater amounts of dopamine in the reward centers in his brain *anticipating joy* through his endless emails, texts, and social technology, I was delaying my happiness and increasing my anxiety levels. I was not aware of this at the time. I could not understand why I was unhappy living in the future while he appeared to be unaffected by the disappointments. Now I know. It was that darned dopamine hormone. In the end, the delayed joy and happiness and fear of the moment resulted in a painful, if necessary, divorce.

Many people avoid Mindful Happiness because they believe somehow that being happy today will distract them, or in some way keep them off their game. *If I focus on being happy now, I won't be focused on planning for the future. I won't get my work completed. I can't stop and think about what is making me happy now because I have to work to get ahead. If I tell people how happy I am, they may not take me seriously.*

I remember when I worked as a school psychologist. After a few months on the job, several coworkers told me I was too happy. As if there is such a thing! My coworkers told me I needed to quit before I became cynical like most of the other psychologists in the office.

There are many people who live with the belief, "don't feel, don't enjoy, just sacrifice and it will lead you to happiness in the end." I am aware of no rule on the books that says you should feel guilty for feeling happy, and yet most of us do. We all live in the rat race of life. Many of us grew up learning at a young age to focus on the work of accomplishment now and enjoy the fruits of our efforts later. My father used to tell me that if you have time to play and enjoy, you have time to work harder. We live in a world that emphasizes rewards, accomplishments, and bank accounts as the vehicles to greater happiness rather than anything internal.

Does this sound familiar?

"As soon as I finish this, I'll have time to be happy."

How is that working for you?

If you use every minute of your waking hours to play catch-up while never taking time to experience some small Mindful Tickle, you really are going to burn yourself out.

Finally, there are those of us who share the belief that you can't allow yourself to be happy if those around you are miserable or in a bad place. It is somehow impolite or bad form. Or have you ever felt of a friend, "She is in a good place, and that's not fair! I'm not happy, why is she?" I can remember after 9-11 when weddings still took place as scheduled and people were feeling guilty about it. Many people felt survivor's guilt, especially those who would normally have been in one of the towers that day but, for a variety of reasons, were not.

I want you to know that it's ok to have a Mindful Tickle even during sad times. When my father passed away, I constantly looked for mindful happiness as a coping mechanism. I knew my father wanted me to be happy. My sister inadvertently provided me with the Mindful Tickle I needed when, in a misguided effort to be fashionable, she wore a pantsuit to the funeral that made her look like a bellhop. The outfit provided Mindful Tickles to all of us – we made 'ding' noises in the background as if summoning her. Even my sister thought it was funny and enjoyed the moment. It was that little bit of present joy that got us through a difficult and sad day.

Let's focus on the benefits we receive by slowing down in order to focus on our present, versus focusing on what we should do next.

When you are happy in the present moment in a way that is not attached to the future, here are some of the benefits you will experience:

- Increased productivity

- Enhanced creativity

- Multiplied joy and happiness

- Positive influences on personal and business life

- Increased emotional and social intelligence

- Expanded influence and leadership abilities with peers and colleagues

- Lowered stress levels

- Increased ability to learn new things

- More patience

- Improved sleep quality

- Boosted immune system

- Expanded circle of friends

- Increased quality of relationships

- Opened brain centers

Mindful Happiness, then, will lead you to increased happiness overall and a more positive lifestyle. The increased pleasure hormones in your brain will raise your mood and motivation levels. You will cultivate compassion for yourself and others. When you find a moment of happiness, it will lower your stress levels and increase your productivity and creativity.

Why Delayed Happiness is Bad for Your Health

We've discussed the benefits of recognizing your happiness in the present. Let's examine the consequences of delaying happiness.

Our state of mind and emotions are an important part of our daily life. When you feel overextended, how does it affect you? I know I feel drained and stressed. Think of how much more productive you feel in your daily life when you are happy. It affects your interaction with people completely. A joyful moment makes you feel more connected with others around you. Conversely, when you are sad or unhappy, you manifest an energy around you that most people will tend to avoid. Working to the point of exhaustion comes at a cost which, in the end, can *hurt*, not help your potential. There is such a thing as *too much work*. It will lower your energy levels, isolate you from family and coworkers, and decrease your resiliency to change.

It's a dangerous myth that you should sacrifice your happiness in the short term for a fulfilled long term. Instead, you become burned out and unengaged, which greatly impacts your relationships.

When all is said and done, hugging your cell phone alone in bed will give you little comfort on a rainy Sunday morning.

The point is clear: stop chasing your future because your happiness should be experienced in the present. Be aware how overthinking increases the potential for unhappiness and makes you more likely to feel powerless and self-critical. Your life will be as joy-filled or as misery-inducing as you want it to be. It all boils down to your relationship with yourself. How do you treat yourself? Would you put up with that kind of treatment from another person? Think about what is joyful *at this moment*. Don't focus on what is annoying you.

When my marriage failed, I had a choice. Should I tell myself that I could never be happy again? Or should I tell myself that my life would never be the same, but that this was a gate opening to a change in my life that could make me happier? Sometimes the single worst thing that happens to us ends up leading to the best outcome.

Can You Be Happy 100% of the Time?

The short answer is simple. No. No one is happy 100% of the time. We must understand that we all define happiness differently. What's important is how *you* define happiness and what you do to make *your* life experience amazing. Studies suggest that 40% of our happiness is within our control. The other percentages are divided into genetics and circumstances.

How to Tickle Your Mind

Here are some helpful thoughts and suggestions to consider as you examine your own happiness. Pick and choose what is right for you. And, most importantly – Enjoy!

Happiness is Not One Size Fits All. Everyone's path to being happy will be different. Set your own priorities and goals for finding your purpose and achieving success, then go for it. But remember, it's not a race. Whatever you do, avoid comparing yourself to others. For example, a friend of mine recently became engaged to the man of her dreams. She is happy and starting a new life. However, her joyful event was an instant trigger for another of our friends to feel sad because she was not in a committed relationship. Stay in your own shoes, my friend.

Give Yourself Permission to Feel Happy. You have the right to be happy. Allow this to happen. It sounds silly to say, but many people just don't feel that they deserve to be happy. They feel as if they have not earned this right. *Hello?* Happiness is NOT an unachievable reward. No matter what the situation or the people around you, you are entitled to be happy.

Life is Short. We Have a Limited Time on This Planet. We shape who we are by our mistakes, regrets, and challenges. Please stop beating yourself up by thinking about what you have done wrong in your life. *Woulda-coulda-shoulda.* Yup, it's a trap. True, I think about my many downfalls, but I can't get into a time machine and fix them. Have I grown from them? Absolutely! That's why I don't want to forget them, and why I can celebrate my mistakes.

There is Much to be Said About Gratitude. Do you have a roof over your head? Something to eat? At least one person in your life? A pair of shoes? A clean bed? Take a minute and write down three things you are grateful for. Much has been taken away in my life: I have learned the hard way not to take my blessings for granted while I have them. Unexpected situations can arise and, without your permission, rob you of the things you treasure. I had much to be grateful for as I pulled up my driveway and saw my entire neighborhood on fire. My family, pets, and neighbors all got out alive. Yes, it was scary, and it displaced us, but all I could do was keep telling myself how grateful I was that we were all safe and alive. Things are just things! More and more will not make you happier.

Just be Happy Without a Reason. Just wake up and think, "I am happy." It can be that simple!

Rate Your Happiness Daily. Where are you in this moment? Don't compare it to other moments. Stay in your present.

Discover Random Acts of Kindness. I love this. Each day I try to do something randomly for someone else. But here's the thing: it has to be completely random and unconditional. It brings joy to my heart to see someone receive an unexpected token of appreciation and acknowledgment. Think of how you feel when someone in your life gives you a hug or sends you a special letter. Clean out your closet and give someone something you admired. Pay the toll for the person behind you. I love to write my Mom a special letter or send her a funny card. Bring the neighborhood fire station some baked goods. Sometimes I randomly hug people I don't know (with permission, of course!) It opens your heart and makes others feel special. I also send my kids at college a 'homesick box' with some of their favorite treats. Random acts of kindness will allow you to appreciate your own good fortunes, make you feel more in control of your life, and build your social connections with others. Being a happy person will bring you more friends. Everyone wants to hang with positive and happy people. Give someone the best gift that's free – your attention!

Acknowledge the Good in Your Life. Focusing on negative will not make you feel better. When you find yourself doing this, write down three good things and focus on them. Explain briefly why you think good things happened on each day. Keep your attention on enduring sources of goodness around you.

Take a Brisk 30-Minute Walk at Least Three Days a Week. Observe sights, sounds, and smells. Make an effort to acknowledge the various sources of joy around you. Being physically active will activate pleasant feelings by increasing endorphins and lower the chances for depression. Endorphins are related to a positive mood and an overall enhanced sense of well-being.

Go for a Car Ride and Turn On Music You Enjoy. Immersing yourself in your favorite tunes while driving through the streets of your neighborhood or surrounding areas can shift your energy and make you feel wonderful.

Listen to Music, Light Candles, Create a Happy Space at Home or Your Work Environment. Surround your environment with pictures or souvenirs that represent happy thoughts and good times. Buy a mug with a happy saying. Reinforce the positive around you. I used to keep a candy dish on my desk. You would be surprised how often co-workers with a sweet tooth visited me throughout the day, and how much of a pick me up these small treats were.

Meditate for at Least 10 Minutes a Day. Studies suggest that meditation permanently rewires your brain and will raise your level of happiness by increasing your gray matter.

Do Something Meaningful. Volunteer your time or call a friend that you have not spoken to for a while. You'd be amazed by how quickly this will improve your mood.

Start a Meaningful Photo Practice. Look at photos that are meaningful to you and reflect upon them, whether they showcase family members, favorite sports, favorite vacation locations, etc. Ask yourself, *what does this photo represent? Why is it meaningful to me?* I keep tons of photos of the love of my life, my dog Murphy! This way, I keep him near me always. I also have a few pictures of my favorite vacation spots and future spots I want to see.

Stop and Take a Breath. Stay in your present. Stop chasing the future and live for the moment. Be mindful. Name one happy thought that puts a smile on your face. Who do you think of when you name a person in your life who is really funny?

Do Nothing. Make time for yourself. It's amazing having the entire house to yourself. DO you put others' happiness ahead of your own? Once upon a time, I was the queen of putting myself last. Not a good idea. You will be happier and more on your mark if you fill yourself up with energy. No one is going to make you happier than you can make yourself. Turn all of your electronics off and enjoy some quiet time. No television, cell phone, or social media, even if just for an hour. I first started with an hour, and now I shoot for an entire day. At first, it can be nerve-wracking. But trust me: in no time at all you will feel energized and happy.

Cultivate Optimism. My son calls this, "making a win." Find a task that no matter what, results in a positive ending. Remember when you were little and you used to buy grab bags or get excited about what was at the bottom of a cereal box? You could not lose. There was ALWAYS a prize at the end. Win and charge onward!

Do More Activities That You Truly Engage In. What activities bring you joy and happiness? Write a list of new activities you can try and a bucket list of joyful events to do. Since we are all individuals with our own preferences, they will vary from person to person. I love concerts. Being around people at a concert always provides me with moments of joy because the mood is always fun and upbeat. Bowling is not my greatest skill, but it makes me laugh. Playing UNO in a large group is also joyful for me. What makes you joyful?

Practice Religion or Spirituality. The active practice of religion and spirituality can connect you with a like-minded community. Prayer can be a form of meditation. Getting to know the divine spark within yourself can help you find the joy and love inside you.

Take Care of Your Body. Your physical well-being can affect your mental well-being. When you feel good physically, you feel good mentally. Get a spa treatment. Try a new haircut. Eat healthy foods, and try to avoid sugar. Feeling good about yourself can make you happy.

Just Be You. Look at yourself in the mirror and give yourself three compliments. Focus on what you like about yourself, not what you don't like. It's best to do this without clothes and alone without an audience.

Surround Yourself with Positive People. Call people you know who tend to have a positive spin on everything. We all have at least one or two friends who seem to find a silver lining in every difficult situation.

Laugh Out Loud and Smile. It seems obvious, but it's easy to forget: this will increase a good mood. And, when you're sad or upset, it will trick your brain into a happier state. So, when you are upset with someone, smile at them. It will change your course of action, and confuse your enemies.

Drink Plenty of Water and Try to Avoid Alcohol. Alcohol is a depressant. Likewise, if you are dehydrated, you may not feel well which will decrease your happiness.

Sleep, Sleep, Sleep. Adequate sleep increases your overall cognitive function. A good quality sleep makes you feel more positive and happier. If you have trouble sleeping, see a doctor. There may be a medical reason that can be cured.

Enjoy Sex. Studies report that sex several times a week will add to your happiness and make you feel more connected to your mate.[5] It also increases those brain hormones!

Buy Something for Someone Else. Buy something tangible for a friend and revel in their response. Or, do as psychologist Martin Seligman suggests: if you spend money on yourself, it should be on an activity, like a trip or a movie.

Fake It. Even when you are not, pretend to be happy. You might just convince yourself!

Engage in a Game You Have Fun Playing. Card games, board games, a puzzle – anything that does not turn into a competition. Find joyful play partners.

Choose an Experience that Makes You Feel Better. Many believe that buying things will not make you feel happy or joyous. This can be true, especially if you compare your purchase to someone else's. For example, if you go shopping with a friend and she buys something more expensive, are you happy with your purchase independently of what she chose? Studies report that purchasing a ticket to a movie or a trip will make you happier over time because the memory will

---

5 "The Happiness Track: How to Apply the Science of Happiness to Accellerate Your Success" Kindle Edition, by Emma Seppala.

remain with you longer than a specific item. Personally, I feel you need to make your own call on this one. My mother always told me to buy a pair of panties whenever I needed to turn my mood around. That in and of itself gives me a Mindful Tickle. I have since made the same recommendation to my own daughter. We are often gleeful shopping at Victoria's Secret. I believe the hunt keeps us both mindful and strengthens our bond when we have an 'off' day.

Mindful Tickles, or moments of joy, help you stay in your present. Even on your most hectic of days, it is important to close your eyes and think of something that puts a smile on your face or a ping of joy in your heart.

Make the practice of Mindful Tickles a daily priority, but don't feel pressured with the task. I guarantee you will find that Mindful Happiness can be contagious. Soon, you too may be chuckling aloud multiple times a day!

CHAPTER THREE

FINDING YOUR LOST MIND

"Flow in the living moment – we are always in a process of becoming and nothing is fixed. Have no rigid system in you, and you'll be flexible to change with the ever changing. Open yourself and flow, my friend. Flow in the total openness of the living moment. If nothing within you stays rigid, outward things will disclose themselves. Moving, be like the water. Still, be like a mirror. Respond like and echo."

~ Bruce Lee

Mindfulness is a term many people in various sectors seem to be throwing around lately. From corporations and businesses, to sports teams and yoga studios, the list goes on and on.

What exactly is mindfulness? And when you're stressed beyond belief and feel as though you are losing your mind, how in the world can you stop and be mindful?

Trust me, I speak from personal experience. I know how hard it is to wrap your mind around this, but I know it can be done. Once you learn how to do it, it can be easy!

I was briefly introduced to mindfulness and meditation for the first time 14 years ago. I was a partner in a nutraceutical company that developed products for pain relief. Much to my surprise, one day I was asked to be our company's spokesperson on QVC, the home shopping channel.

Although from the audience's perspective it looks like a fun job, representing the product on television was beyond stressful. I was live on the air, with all sorts of people – directors, legal professionals, etc. – talking to me through an earpiece. I had to listen to them while taking calls from potential customers and talking to them, too. To top it off, I could not ignore the glaring monitors that kept tallying my sales.

Did I mention that I only had three to five minutes of airtime? Everyone was depending on me to get the job done quickly and efficiently, and yet I had to smile and look relaxed. Prior to going on, I'd written all of my important talking points on my hand, which turned out to be a bad idea, since I was promoting a liquid product. My notes quickly washed off as I demonstrated how our product worked.

The best part of that experience was meeting a famous Hollywood actress and business woman in the green room who had tons of experience on QVC. I was eager to learn from her experiences. She advised me to learn about meditation and mindfulness and referred me to the Chopra Center in San Diego. At the time, with a career and two kids to raise, I didn't have the time or funds to enroll in many classes. How could I find the time to read Dr. Chopra? And what was mindfulness anyway?

Years later, when my life seemed to be totally falling apart in every way possible, someone again informed me about the benefits of mindfulness. I was distraught, fearful of my future, and desperate for answers. My head felt as though I could not handle one more problem or it would fall to the floor. A shell of my former self, my energy was depleted. I was desperate to find something to help me find my way. Could this be the thing that worked?

With nothing to lose, I began to investigate mindfulness. It started with trying to get an understanding of where I was. I was feeling mindlessness, experiencing brain overload, and doing too much at one time. In order to make a change, I first had to understand my own process. I had to get to know my own mind.

We All Have "Mindless" Moments.

Have you ever driven home from work and as you're pulling into the driveway, you start to wonder how you could possibly be home already? You don't seem to remember anything about the ride, whether stopping at red lights or passing by the familiar streets that line your usual route home.

Or have you ever gone out to dinner with friends or family and, after a great discussion, realized that you have eaten your entire meal without being able to recall taking more than a bite or two?

In both of these examples, our brains have transitioned into what I call *"Mindlessness."* Our mind is fixated on so many thoughts and stimuli around us in our chaotic lives that we are not present and aware of what is going on in the here and now.

Somehow, in these situations, our brains take over like an airplane's autopilot system. Although autopilot will get you where you need to go safely, you will miss out on much along the way. Think about the first scenario I described: as you sat behind the steering wheel of your car and drove home. You remained unaware on a conscious level of the other cars and people around you – not to mention the bright rainbow ahead. In the case of the dinner party, you missed out on the sensory experience of eating delicious food. You may also miss warning signals.

What else are you missing due to a lack of awareness? What are you not observing from your co-workers or family members by not being in the present?

After my own life fell completely apart, it took years for me to understand the extent of what I had missed. I missed red flags and health issues, I misread emotions, failed to feel joy, and experienced many miscommunications. Stories I had never previously questioned no longer made sense to me. My mind was so overloaded that I could not hear myself think, let alone listen to my inner voice. Filled with anxiety and self-doubt, I had neglected my all-important gut instinct.

Most of us live in a mindless or *mind-filled* existence. In general, we were raised in families whose central beliefs included success through hard work, defined by financial success. You probably heard that relaxation was for slackers, not high achievers. In order to meet or exceed the expectations of others, in order to be noticed, it was necessary to work late.

We are a society of social-climbers, multi-taskers, and social media addicts. We are chained to our smartphones, Fitbits, and other complicated modern technology.

Guess what?

Our brains and bodies were not designed for multi-tasking and all of today's physical wear and tear. When you are feeling overloaded and overwhelmed in your life, it signals your brain to be on the defensive.

How often do you wake up with the "wrong side of the bed" syndrome? For some unknown reason, you have morning dread, feeling grumpy and irritated. Thanks to a good night's sleep, you feel like you should have awakened wide-eyed and bushy tailed. Yet, before you even get out of bed to start your day, you feel overwhelmed and stressed. Believe it or not, this is common. One more thing to blame on our brains.

Some mornings, upon awakening, we have the highest levels of the stress hormone cortisol in our blood for the entire day. This extra shot of cortisol can trigger us to immediately start the "Oh, no!" anxious thinking about the overload of tasks we are facing before we put one foot on the floor. To add insult to injury, our defense mechanisms are still sluggish, which adds to our stressful start-up. It will take time and a lot of effort on the part of our body to lower those levels.

Does this mean you should just stay in bed? No, of course not. We will discuss ways to reduce cortisol in the next chapter. For now, it's just important to understand that our physiology contributes to our stress levels; it's not just in our heads, it's in our hormones.

I think most of us can agree that two common goals we all share include being happy and successful no matter how we define those things. In this pursuit of happiness and success, we must also deal with the pace of our lives reaching overwhelming and unpredictable levels. We have allowed advances in our technology to run our daily existence.

When you reach into your purse to retrieve your cell phone, and it's not there, do you feel a sense of panic or relief? I have watched panicked people tear up a room looking for a missing phone. In that moment, they lost all sense of perspective. Their entire world is turned upside down.

Every day we face pressing deadlines and endless tasks. When we're not checking emails, texts, social media accounts, cell phone messages, and work phones, we're reading blogs, news reports, and stock market updates. All of this has to fit into the necessary tasks of preparing meals, making grocery lists, attending social events, taking care of after-school issues with kids, and planning time with our spouses. It is never ending.

In modern times, there is an abundance of information at our disposal, which becomes a double-edged sword. We can research any topic, locate any restaurant, even find a date online. The benefits seem endless. However, this easy access also comes with a steep price.

We are conditioned to expect instant gratification in the form of immediate responses to our calls, texts, and emails. Many of us get frustrated if 10 minutes go by without a response. How did our parents survive communication via snail mail? Once upon a time, before FedEx and telephones, people had to wait days or more for the exchange of correspondence. In our 21st Century society, when that response is delayed, our first thought is often negative. We fear – or even assume – something has gone wrong. We treat our phones like a beloved family member, always with us, night and day. We even sleep with our cell phones right next to us. Staying in touch with the world is the first thing we do in the morning and our last task before signing off for the night.

Amid all this activity, we never seem to have a chance to unplug from the world. Most of us have accepted 'overextension' as a way of life. We crave the acceptance of others. We strive to be good parents, spouses, employees, and bosses. To make that happen, we just keep moving forward while we push the limits of our own well-being. In the end, this leads not to success, but to burnout, heightened stress levels, unsatisfactory relationships, and an internal disconnect. With so much demand on our time and attention, the myth that this type of success will bring us happiness backfires.

In reality, all of the rushing and straining prompted by the unrelenting need to keep up inevitably leads to self-blame and sadness. We tell ourselves that we must not be working hard enough because we're not fulfilling all of our responsibilities and our dreams haven't come true. Maybe we are too frazzled to realize that our unwavering focus on competition, activity, and multitasking may be hindering our success. Too many of us have bought into the myth that 'idleness is bad.'

Not only are we feeling overwhelmed by technology, but think about this: our brains are constantly bombarded with information. In fact, we receive over 11 million bits of information per second. Wow, right? My head hurts just thinking about it! These bits of information enter our brain through our senses – mostly through our eyes and ears. Thank goodness we have a tendency to focus on only about seven at a time. The remaining millions of bits that stay in our subconscious awareness can still play a role in our thinking and behaviors.

We react to these seven different bits in one of three ways: like, dislike, or neutral. We like compliments, positive feedback, good food, a great parking spot, commuting without traffic, and leaving work early. We dislike mean-spirited gossip, flat tires, unexpected changes to our schedules, additional work assignments, and rainy days without umbrellas. It's human nature to prefer the things we like to the things we dislike. When we like something, we produce more dopamine, which reinforces the desire to like things. We are hooked on dopamine neurotransmitters and the signals they make between our brain cells. Dopamine rewards us by making us feel instant joy and fulfillment. When we are getting what we want, here comes the dopamine. We like it. It's yummy, and we want more.

This is why we love our cell phones and the myriad of positive stimuli on it. It's immediate gratification we can look at any time. Look who 'likes' our posts – look who wants to talk to us! It's a constant dopamine supplier. But there's a downside to dopamine. We can become addicted to it. It is what leads us to addictions like drug abuse or gambling. Because we spend most of our lives heavily influenced by rewards from other people, we allow our surroundings to provide us with daily shots of dopamine. In the next few chapters, you will learn how you can make changes in your life and better regulate your dopamine cravings without changing your surroundings.

As we are discussing the overextension of our brains, I would be remiss not to include the topic of multitasking. First and foremost, our brains are not wired to multitask. When you are working on two tasks at the same time, your brain must quickly shift your attention from one task to the other. It cannot focus attention on both at the same time. For example, when you are emailing while talking to a client on the phone, your attention switches on your computer while you are writing the email, then off, before switching on again to focus on what your client is saying. This may happen in rapid succession, which can be exhausting. Every time we switch our attention from one task to another, it takes energy and time away from the brain, because it requires an increase of mental effort from you.

We've all been overstimulated. For example, when a call comes in at the same time someone is standing in front of you making a request, it is difficult for our brain to do its jobs efficiently while juggling. In addition, our brains are also simultaneously regulating our emotions. Picture yourself, when you are attempting to multitask, as a juggler in a circus. At any moment, all the balls could come crashing down. Just keeping them in the air takes all your effort, leaving you with nothing left for anything else.

I used to believe that by multitasking I could fit so much more into my jam-packed day. When I was at home, it was hard for me to focus on one task at a time. In fact, I could never understand why my husband could not do at least two or three things at the same time in the kitchen. I often called people as I swept the floor or did the dishes. I never realized it was taking me double the amount of time. Multitasking damages our productivity and exhausts us. Ultimately, it adds more time to our tasks. Research reports multitasking takes 30 percent longer, and we are likely to make twice the number of errors compared to completing one task at a time.[6] Multitasking also lowers the quality of our decision making. Therefore, we make poorer choices when we multitask.

You may not realize it, but when you take your personal phone to the office, you increase the chances that you are training your brain to expect to multitask. Each time you feel the vibration or hear the ping of your phone, your dopamine breaks into a happy dance and signals your brain that new information is coming. The uncertainty of the email, text, or message sends a small surge of dopamine which is hard for us to ignore. However, our brain's working memory is extremely limited – these small distractions can make it harder to concentrate and burn more of your mental energy. The same thing can also happen when performing one task if you're constantly distracted by your thoughts.

If you are writing a report at work while thinking about what you need to be doing next, you are distracting yourself from concentrating on the task at hand. Just remember, each time you are distracted or interrupted, it will take you between 10 to 15 minutes to regain your train of thought. On any given day, you can begin to calculate the time lost by the number of interruptions and the pings of your phone.

---

6 Rasmus Hougaard and Jacqueline Carter, "One Second Ahead: Enhance Your Performance at Work with Mindfulness" November 3, 2015

The only exception to doing more than one thing at a time would be a task that requires no conscious thought from you. For example, I walk my dog and return phone calls at night. As long as I am walking on the same path or don't run into unexpected animals on my trail, I am able to focus on my conversation and walk at the same time.

So now we understand why **SINGLE BRAIN TASKS** work best. It takes less brain power, mental effort, and time to get all our work finished. I also know why I love the pings on my phone with an incoming message. They provide a powerful shot of dopamine. When I am not working, I try to put my brain in a resting state, which is the best way I can enhance my learning and insight.

Try this brief exercise:

Stop for a second. Close your eyes for two minutes. What are you thinking about? Are you quiet internally and not thinking anything? Are you thinking about work? Or maybe a grocery list, or what you are going to do later?

My world so often felt overwhelming and chaotic. I thought it would be easier for me to identify my 'mind filled' world by writing a mind filled list.

Here is just a sample of what would be swirling around in my brain at any given moment before I became mindful:

- Worrying
- Explaining
- Giving emotional support to my son and daughter
- My ability to give financial support to my son and daughter
- Email
- Daily texting
- A feeling of being overwhelmed
- Having to rush

- Stress
- Trying to multitask
- My commute
- A feeling of exhaustion
- Planning my daily exercise
- Procrastinating
- Shopping
- Cooking
- Preparing for work
- Writing a book
- Catching up with friends and family
- Dating
- Getting my 8 glasses of water a day
- Walking the dogs
- Getting the kids' needs met
- Getting dressed
- Waiting
- Pretending all is well
- Hoping for the best
- Concern about my future
- Completing work tasks on time
- Ignoring the negativity around me
- Concerns regarding my Mother's health

Write your own list of typical thoughts and concerns passing through your mind today.

Now that we know what mind-LESS-ness is, in the next chapter, we will define mind-FULL-ness.

CHAPTER FOUR

AN EMPTY MIND LEADS TO MIND-FULL-NESS

"You are what you pay attention to because attention is like a spotlight in a vacuum cleaner – it illuminates what it rests upon, and then it sucks it into your brain."
~ Rick Hanson, Ph.D.

I don't know about you, but when my mind is full, and I constantly feel hammered by my daily dose of craziness, I can barely keep my eyes open past 9 p.m. My chronic mind-speediness wears on my body in bad ways, like weakening my immune system and dragging down my mood. It also puts my brain on constant high alert, which results in my finding more things to worry about or becoming irritable quicker.

Our neurochemistry can lead to changes in our mood, thoughts, concentration, patience, feelings, desires, memory, and resilience. From a neurological perspective, this puts our brains are on a never-ending idling merry-go-round with the consequence of our loss of the ability to stay in the present.

If I asked you to write a list of the things that you did for yourself this week, what would they include?

Maybe you went to the gym, got a manicure, bought a new pair of shoes, or had lunch with a friend. But at any point during this busy week, did you take the time to give your mind a rest? A strange inquiry, right? But is it? During your manicure, did you make chit-chat with the nail technician? Or look at a magazine? At the gym, were you talking to friends? Watching TV on the treadmill? Thinking about what to make for dinner or how much laundry you had to do?

When your feet are tired after a long walk, you sit down and rest your tired toes! But when was the last time you took 10 minutes out of your day and sat in a comfortable chair and did nothing? Undisturbed silence. No phone, no electronics, no eating, conversations, reading, working, or TV. Simply nothing, no thoughts about the past or planning for the future.

I can tell you very honestly, I never gave it a second thought until just over a decade ago. Even after taking all of my neuroscience classes, it didn't cross my mind. Not one professor mentioned giving the mind a rest. Yet our mind is our everything. It is a huge asset. Think of all the tasks that our mind does. It keeps us emotionally stable (or makes us unstable!), it makes us feel happy (or unhappy!). We depend upon our mind for productivity, creativity, spontaneity, focus, and clarity. Among other things, of course.

It's ironic that we are so worried about our weight or feeling physically healthy, but we have little concern for our most valid asset. I believe that most people think that when you sleep your brain magically shuts down and rests. This is a misconception. Your brain is remarkably active while you sleep.

Now that you are aware of the need for your mind to rest, are you willing to give it a try?

One of the main reasons I wanted to write this book was to help people – people like you – change their minds through mindfulness, just as I did mine. I will explain the tools you need to make that happen. By the time you finish reading this, you will have the transformative power to recharge and rewire your mind. When someone told me I could change my life by being still for 10 minutes, twice a day, I thought it was ridiculous. Probably in the same way that you think it is ridiculous as you are reading this. But I promise you this: training your attention requires patience and practice, but it is so worth it.

Change Your Mind, Change Your Life

The automatic stress response, along with the physiological response, increases a stress hormone called cortisol. Cortisol's job is to trigger adrenaline increases that start a shift in your body's response, with negative consequences including, but not limited to: inflammation, infertility, insomnia, heart palpitations, muscle loss, infertility, and increased cholesterol. No matter how big or how small the life stressors, our brains all react in the same way. If you are worried about getting fired, not having enough money to retire, or whether or not you turned off your curling iron at home, your brain fires the same exact hormones. That 'fight or flight' rush begins with the almond and the seahorse asking the frontal lobes for commentary and analysis and alerting the stress hormones (epinephrine, norepinephrine, and cortisol) which affect our bodies and emotions.

If these responses are all automatic and below our consciousness, you may wonder how we could possibly change anything about this. Here's how:

In the beginning, when huge, dangerous creatures chased us as prey, we either ran or stayed to fight. Once the threat passed, our bodies returned to the normal state. Our parasympathetic nervous system kicked in and allowed 'resting and digesting' of critical information.[7] It allowed us to rest afterwards, and properly sort through the information we learned during the stressful situation.

This part is critical. We need to stop and slow down after a stressor so we can regain our strength and recover. In modern times, who does that? No one. Instead, we move on to the next task, the next worry, the

---

7 Our parasympathetic nervous system is a much slower system that moves along longer neural pathways. It is responsible for controlling homeostasis, or, the balance and maintenance of the body's systems. It restores the body to a state of calm and counterbalance and allows it to relax and repair.

next stressor. We simply allow our chronic stress levels to keep building up inside of us.

As difficult as it can be for most of us, we all need to sit back and examine our lifestyles. And, if we are brutally honest, we'll agree that our stress is often the result of out-of-control thinking. We've allowed the recordings in our brains to control us. But it isn't the stressor that is doing damage to us – it is our reaction to it. What we tell ourselves affects what we see, and what we see affects what we feel. When we are stressed out, we tend not to see the entire picture clearly. We do not evaluate the facts as they are. Instead, we think about past experience, our anxiety for the future, and our demands about how things should be. All of this gets layered on top of the present set of events. In that moment, we can't use the part of the brain that keeps us engaged in the present. Face it: when we are stressed, we are less empathetic to others and harder on ourselves.

The parasympathetic system opposes our 'fight or flight' reflex. As a result, the resting, digesting, and healing can't take place when our survival hormones are running. The biochemistry of resting and digesting are critical for survival, too, but for long-term survival. Nature can give you a spurt of urgency, but it can't give you a spurt of relaxation. If stress mode has been your preferred way of being, you will have to make a conscious effort to slow down and heal.

Given what we know, how can we stop the brain's almond (amygdala) response? How do we get to the 'resting and digesting' place?

Mindfulness training is one of the best ways to handle your life's daily overload and mental chatter. Before we delve into the benefits of mindfulness and how it can change your life, let's make sure we understand what mindfulness means.

Mindfulness is staying in your present. It is an emotionally non-reactive state. It's the here and now. You are not 'past looping' and thinking of the past, nor are you 'future tripping' and thinking ahead. It is the art of learning to pay attention to the here and now. You have the ability to contemplate what is going on in your mind in the present moment without running with it. You can feel emotions or sensations without an attached story. In this state, you do not allow your emotions to take control over you, while you observe what is in front of you without judgment. Your responses are infused with compassion, not fear, negativity, or insecurity. When thoughts about the past or future come to us and take us away from our present experience, and we get 'lost in thought' we try to notice this and force ourselves to return to the now. By purposely directing our awareness away from the hijacking thoughts and back to the stillness, we decrease the effect they have on our lives, and we start the process of clarity and calmness.

During the present experience, don't judge whether what you are experiencing is good or bad. If those thoughts appear, let them go. If they won't go on their own, kick them out. Don't get upset because you are feeling something you don't want to be experiencing or because you are not experiencing what you would rather be experiencing. Accept whatever arises. Observe it. Notice it, arising, passing through, and finally leaving. Think of yourself as sitting in a bus station, watching the buses come and go. You don't have any opinion about the buses – they simply arrive at the station, you notice them, and then they leave. It doesn't matter if they are shiny new buses, or buses in poor mechanical shape, they are simply buses. Those buses are your thoughts. They come, they go. They are not to be judged. Good or bad thoughts or feelings simply exist: stay neutral, non-reactive. Your mind is still and balanced.

Mindfulness training was developed thousands of years ago, but its definition and applications have transitioned over time. It's not a religion. It requires no faith or belief and does not conflict with any religious belief. Anyone can enjoy its benefits – they are similar to, and in many ways not different than, prayer. Mindfulness does not take all of life's pressures away: it is a way of reacting to life's pressures. It helps us respond to them in a calmer state. It also gives us a chance to pull back and recognize our unconscious emotional and physiological reactions to life's everyday challenges. Mindfulness is a tool that allows us to pay attention, so we can clearly see what is happening in our lives and what our bodies are telling us.

In basic terms, mindfulness means thinking in the present. When you're in the practice of mindfulness, there is only one now; your thoughts are not focused on the past or engaging in fantasies of the future. Instead, you are concentrating on one object of choice, for as long as you want, with minimal effort. You are fully present with the people in front of you or the one task at hand.

To be mindful is to actually feel the sensations in your body – even the unpleasant ones – without clinging to them or wishing them away. Yup, your foot is asleep. Notice that. Now, let that thought go. Just return to the present moment over and over again, even as your thoughts relentlessly try to take you away from it. You are living in the moment and in a state of active, open attention! Remember our minds wander, on average, 50% of the time. It's a common experience.

Consider this: between 47% and 50% of our thoughts in a day are on autopilot. We are just going through the motions of life during those times. Half of your life is lost in thoughts stressing you out, often leading to unhappiness. I don't know about you, but I don't want half of my life to be unhappy.

Scientific research [8]reports that staying in your present moment will increase your sense of happiness overall. In fact, the sense of happiness stays with you if you stay in your present even when you are doing something you dislike. Sometimes I sit and look outside my window at the water and enjoy seeing the reflection of the light on the water. It looks like diamonds. I smile, and I feel grateful. Or, perhaps I could sit in a chair and think

---

8 Eileen Luders, et al., "The Underlying Anatomical Correlates of Long-Term Meditation: Larger Hippocampal and Frontal Volumes of Gray Matter." Neuroimage 45 (2009) 672-78.

about what I am going to do when I retire and wonder if I will have the means to do it. Do I have full control over my future? No. So why keep stressing out about the future?

Dr. John Kabat-Zinn, the founder of the Center for Mindfulness at the University of Massachusetts, has this to say:

"Mindfulness refers to the experiencing of our thoughts, feelings, and physical sensations as they are in the here and now, without judging them and without actively trying to change them. Thus, when you mindfully drop into your own inner dialogue, the quality of your self-examination is less judgmental because you are not labeling it as good, bad, distorted, or not distorted. When you are mindful, it's easier to recognize when your automatic thoughts are tending in a dangerous direction."[9]

Mindfulness can be a complicated concept to understand. What helps me better grasp the concept is to think of it as a pit stop. All of us need to take a few minutes out of our day to recharge and reflect. We can't work non-stop without any breathing time if we want to remain physically and mentally healthy. Downtime is just as important as any other daily activity. For many, it is hard to wrap your head around the possibility of just allowing your mind to sit idly. I know when I first tried, it made me anxious. What a challenge it was to shut off my thoughts about my to-do list, work, worries, my kids, what to cook for dinner, and so on. I resisted the necessity of finding 10 or 20 minutes a day. *How could sitting for a short period of time help my brain, when I could use that time to get things done?* I barely had time for a bathroom break, much less time to sit and do nothing.

Wired to just keep moving, I questioned the productivity of mindfulness in my fast-paced daily routine. I had no clue that I would increase my creativity and productivity by making time for stillness and

9 Guided Mindfulness Meditation: A Complete Guided Mindfulness Meditation Program from Jon Kabat-Zinn, Sept 1, 2005 by Jon Kabat-Zinn, PhD.

silence. The problem for me was re-learning how to be idle. I grew up believing that stillness was a sign of laziness. But really, empty space is one of our greatest luxuries in life. It gives your imagination time to breathe.

Operating full-time with a full brain prevents you from receiving subtle signals. It's like trying to have a meaningful conversation in a crowded, noisy restaurant. You have to quiet your mind in order to receive greater insights and creativity. Complex problem-solving works best by stopping and thinking in order for new solutions to come through.

Mindfulness is the simple act of sitting still. This simple act can transform our complicated, demanding, and unique life challenges in the workplace and the home. According to Jack Kornfield, author of *A Lamp in the Darkness: Illuminating the Path Through Difficult Times*, "The present moment is all that we have, and it becomes the doorway to true calm, your healing refuge. The only place that you can love, heal, or awaken is here and now. Create a life a day at a time."

When I am sitting at my desk gazing at the water, I note the stillness, observe the blue sky, and look at the cloud formations. I feel the warm breeze coming through the window and touching my cheek. In that moment, I am not thinking about emails, fearing why the stock market went down today, or wondering if I will have a date this coming weekend – or ever again!

When I think of mindfulness, I think of children and animals. Ever notice when a puppy gets a new toy? They start at it as if the toy was coming to them. They smell it, taste it, bite it, bark at it. Then they stare at it some more, walk with it, bite it again, pull the stuffing out, and play with it. As they fully enjoy the experience, nothing and no one else matters. They are wrapped up in the present, filled with peace and joy. They are completely engrossed in themselves. The same principle applies to young children, who can sit and play with their toys for long periods of time, focusing their attention on the little figures around them. In that moment, they are not thinking about the past or their future. Just the here and now, in their own time and space. It's hard to imagine that we were once that age and practiced stillness so naturally.

When I moved from the West Coast to the East Coast, being mindful was much easier. Everything around me was so new and different. I took long walks just noticing the various plants, trees, grass, and wildlife. Even the colors and textures amazed me. No palm trees! The water was green, warm, and murky in comparison to where I'd lived previously. All of my senses had so much to take in. The sights, sounds, and aroma of nature replaced my frenetic thinking.

My quest for understanding mindfulness was often frustrating. At first, I heard people talking about mindfulness, while others spoke about meditation. Were they the same thing? What makes them different? Can anyone do it? Where can I learn it? Is it best to learn one-on-one or in a group? How long does it take? How will I know if I am doing it correctly? I was curious and filled with unanswered questions. Although the information is more readily available now in 2017 than it was over a decade ago, I would highly recommend using a professional certified meditation trainer.

The terms 'meditation' and 'mindfulness' are often used interchangeably, and sometimes, if used in simplified ways, share a general meaning, which refers to the resting of the mind. Depending on whom you ask, they can even overlap and complement one another. For me, mindfulness is a form of meditation. Whether it is done formally or informally, it involves bringing your full mind at an object or being aware of everything that you do. Meditation is the practice of reaching ultimate consciousness and concentration, to acknowledge the mind and then self-regulate it.

A common form of mindfulness is being aware of your breath during meditation. Since we can choose to focus our attention on an infinite number of objects or ideas, there are many types of mindfulness meditations. If you are focused on your breathing to transcend your ego and touch your inner divinity, you are engaging in basic meditation. If you are focused on your breath for the purpose of holding your attention and training your mind in a non-judgmental way, you are practicing mindfulness.

You may have heard some negative concepts around the idea of mindfulness, so I want to dispel the most common myths of mindfulness.

The Myths of Mindfulness:

- You can only learn to meditate in a Buddhist church or travel to the Far East.

- Anyone can teach you to meditate.

- Mindfulness is part of a cult or religion.

- Mindfulness will reduce your competitive drive or ambition. People at work will perceive you as 'soft.'

- If people discover that you use mindful techniques, it will lower the chances of good job prospects.

- You can't meditate if you think too much.

- You are not supposed to have any thoughts while you meditate.

- You can't meditate because you will never know whether you are doing it correctly.

- Meditation is only useful for people who are stressed out.

- Meditation is only for adults.

- You can't meditate without buying a mantra.

- It will take you years to learn how to meditate.

- Meditation is like sleeping.

- Meditation is just relaxation.

- Meditation will make me 'zone out' during the workday.

I had the honor and privilege of attending mediation training with Sarah McLean, author of *Soul-Centered: Transform Your Life in 8 Weeks with Meditation (Hay House 2012)*. According to Sarah, there are five essentials to mediation. Let's explore them:

1. It's Ok to Have Thoughts When You Meditate. Your mind has endless thoughts. It would be impossible to turn them off as easily as you shut off your water. It does not work that way. You cannot stop thoughts by not thinking about thinking. Initially, I gave up meditation because I could not stop my thoughts. I had no clue that it was a normal process. It is a common concern for the vast majority of people I have trained. When we are still, it becomes obvious that our rambunctious minds are well-trained to dwell in the past and travel to the future. In time, however, the rapid chatter will gradually decrease, and you will experience the quieter levels of your thoughts. Even seasoned monks will tell you they are faced with occasional mental chatter. There is a lot of stored stress and anxiety in that mind of yours: chatter is one of the many ways the body will release it. For example, the first time I went on a cruise ship, the whole first day I was pacing, irritable and bored. I was so used to working two stressful jobs and experiencing sleepless nights as a new mother that I could not relax. As I sat in a chair by the pool sipping a drink, I thought about my to-do list that was waiting for me when I returned to the office. Gradually, I settled in, and, by the last day, I was noticeably more relaxed and calm.

2. **Don't Try Too Hard.** Meditation is not about doing it right or wrong. The experience of meditation is a NATURAL PROCESS. If you are worrying endlessly about whether or not you are doing it right, there is a problem. The more you are concentrating on those thoughts, the more you are thinking instead of being still. You are creating bad habits that way. Remember: you are trying to lessen your stress, not increase it. If you feel as if you should be

assessing your performance, you are only adding to your anxiety. This defeats the entire process. Meditation is a natural, effortless act when done properly. As Sarah points out, the only effort involved is setting the time and space for your regular practice. It's best to be as consistent as you can on this point.

3. **Let Go of Expectations.** Enter the process without any preconceived notions. While meditating, your experiences will vary. You can sit in a chair straight up. Or you can sit cross-legged on a cushion on the floor. You could lie down. What's important here is not how you sit, but that you go into each practice session as if it were the first – with innocence and no expectations. Some practices will be better than others. But that's ok, too. Just welcome whatever feelings or sensations arrive.

4. **Be Kind to Yourself.** Remember the end game here. Your goal for this practice is to be happier, more calm, have better clarity, and to have a better sense of self. Getting down on yourself is creating a bad habit. Each experience is a little bit different. Different: not better or worse. Some days you will have more thoughts or chatter, and some you may have none at all. Other days you will be meditating for 45 minutes, and it will only feel like five minutes.

5. **Stick with It.** This is called a "practice" for a reason. It will take time and patience. But here's the thing: if you stick with it every day for 10 minutes for eight weeks, consistently, you will not believe how much your life will change for the better. In more ways than I can name. Obviously, I love to meditate. At first, however, and even every so often nowadays, it takes discipline. I meditate at least twice a day. In the morning, I get quietly out of bed, go into the bathroom, and then go and sit in my favorite chair. I turn on my timer for 20 minutes, and I start the process. Some days, I am interrupted by my dog who wants to go outside and play. Other times I am interrupted by my children who are

leaving early and need something from me. The phone may ring. Distractions are to be expected. But, once I start, I stay, no matter what the distraction. I stay with it until the end. I have gone so far as to teach my dogs the word "meditate." Believe it or not, they lie next to me peacefully when I give them that "command." On rare occasions, I have found it necessary to lock myself in the car to meditate. No matter how my day goes, I find some sort of time to rest that mind of mine. The trick is to start off with small chunks of time. Build up slowly, so you don't get discouraged and skip it. Even five minutes is better than nothing.

Here is one of my favorite quotes from the Dalai Lama:

"There are always problems to face, but it makes a difference if our minds are calm. On the surface we may get upset, but it makes a difference if we are able to stay calm in the depths of our minds."

This really brings home the point of mindfulness. Even though we live in a NEED FOR SPEED world, we can slow it down and take a breath. The surface isn't what matters – what is in our brains matters. This small change can really change your life.

Meditation and Mindfulness can bring amazing positive impacts and benefits to our lives. Staying in the present allows you to observe all of the things going on around you and within yourself. It allows you to witness your emotions without judgment and with a relaxed mind. Otherwise, we may sometimes become overwhelmed and swept away by our feelings.

Regular, sustained Mindfulness strengthens our attention areas of the brain and changes the way we think and behave. Studies have reported that if you bring mindfulness to your life for at least 27 minutes a day consistently over an eight-week period, it will strengthen your PFC (prefrontal cortex).[10] This results in more effective decision-making, increased self-awareness, compassion, and flexible thinking.

To me, the development of Mindfulness and how it impacts your life is like a fine wine. It's transformational. It allows you to slowly develop from an over-extended, distracted mind to pure focused awareness. It's a slow building progression of self-awareness. As you consistently meditate, the chatter and the external distractions become fewer and fewer. They are replaced by a better understanding of ourselves and our hearts. As your inner peace evolves, you will be happier, connected with yourself and others, and become more compassionate. What a great time to find this amazing tool, when life seems to be crazier and more unpredictable!

---

10 "Buddha's Brain: The Practical Neuroscience of Happiness, Love, and Wisdom." November 1, 2009 by Rick Hanson and Daniel J. Siegel.

CHAPTER FIVE

MIND TOOLS 1.0

"Meditation brings wisdom; lack of meditation brings ignorance. Know well what leads you forward and what holds you back and choose the path that leads to wisdom."
~Buddha

"Meditation is not a matter of trying to stop thinking or make your mind go blank, but rather to realize when your attention is wandering and to simply let go of the thoughts and begin again. It is a way of changing our relationship to our thoughts, so we're not so consumed by them, with no sense of space. Having a newly spacious relationship to our thoughts brings both peace and freedom."
~Sharon Salzberg

Initially, I wanted to learn to meditate as a stress reducer. I had no clue about the other benefits I would also receive. I had no real preconceived notions about the whole process. I just knew I was stressed beyond what I could handle. My mother constantly informed me that "no cross was too big to bear" and "God will only give you the stress that you can handle."

I also knew that my acquaintences on both coasts who regularly meditated seemed very chill and happy. Certainly happier than I was. I remember I went to a seminar in La Costa near my home in California. Deepak Chopra was describing his experience with meditation. He noted that he meditates for two hours a day. I could not take my eyes off his radiant skin. He glowed from the inside out. I wanted to look like that, too!

Yet I was still unclear *how* to meditate, and what I was supposed to do or feel. We sat with Mr. Chopra for ten minutes, quiet except for the repetition of a mantra. Then we opened our eyes. Um, ok...was that it? I was still stressed and unclear about the point of the entire exercise. Still, I kept it up.

It seemed to take forever for me to go deeper into myself. I slowly became less reactive and more responsive in my daily activities. I started a process of change in my life. A bell started going off in my mind – hello, Cynthia! I began to have a better understanding of my life and to recognize that there were some things I simply could not control. But, there were other things that I could control. As the Serenity Prayer says, the wisdom is in knowing the difference.

When I hit D.C. traffic heading home, I can't make everyone get out of my way. Nor can I control the weather on a snowy day so that I can catch a flight on time. However, I can control the way that I react. In my mindful self-discovery, I learned a lot about myself and my patterns of behavior. I found that I had a habit of quickly assessing a situation and making a judgment. This increased my anxiety and stress levels and left me feeling sad. We all do this, right? And we blame our anxiety and stress on the situation. But here's the truth – it isn't the situation that's to blame, it's how we choose to respond to the situation.

And so, I sat still in a comfortable position for 20 minutes. I closed my eyes and said to myself, "Don't think." I repeated my mantra over and over. "Mantra" is a Sanskrit word that means an instrument for the mind. When we talk about a mantra, we mean a sound, word, or short phrase that has meaning to you in a spiritually uplifting way, repeated over and over. My mantra is, "I am clearing." I kept repeating this phrase, yet I couldn't quit thinking about lists and people and emotions. Yes, this is absolutely normal. And yes, it can be frustrating. Meditation is a process in which you are supposed to be aware of your wandering thoughts in your mind. So you are actually on the right track when this happens.

It's all about awareness at this stage. Your mind is not going to stay still for 20 minutes straight as a newbie. Instead, your mind is going to be drawn again and again into thoughts, sounds, smells, and emotions. It will feel like your mind is everywhere except in the present where you want it to be. You soon realize that you are not in control of your mind, not matter what you previously thought.

In order to notice that your mind has wandered, you have to be aware of what it is doing in the first place. This awareness is the start of a good thing. Through awareness, we begin to see life through a bigger lens. We are coming into a greater consciousness. Getting rid of all the recordings in our mind, we are freeing up space for our minds to roam.

I have never stopped training throughout this journey. As I embarked on it, as I rode the rails, and even today, I am constantly bringing my attention back to the present moment. This back and forth is cultivating FOCUS. You will be amazed at how much excessive thinking about the past and future is in your head. Attention is trainable. Practice being mindful and you will gain control over your attention.

Over time, this increased ability to concentrate will keep you more even-tempered less distracted. You will be, in a word, joyful.

Within a month of a consistent meditation practice, I felt more relaxed. My kids also noticed that I was calmer and happier. I was more empathetic. I was more thoughtful and kind to myself and my body. I could sense the energy of the people around me and was less reactive when conflicts surfaced. Over time, I became more aware of my repeated thought patterns, emotions, and bodily responses.

Keep the following in mind as we get into examples of meditation and mindfulness exercises: the practice of meditation is exactly that. It is a practice. Like any exercise, you have to evaluate what practice is best for you. You have to go at your own pace. If you try too hard or for too long you will burn out or get frustrated. There is no special attire. You can wear whatever you would like. I would make the recommendation to wear comfortable, loose-fitting clothes. If you wear something tight or itchy, it may distract you. I like wearing socks because my feet are always cold.

If you are picking a mindfulness exercise that requires sitting, you can sit in a chair or use a cushion on the floor. Meditation cushions can be found for sale. They are specially designed to raise you up when you are in a lotus position and lessen the chance of your foot falling asleep. But you don't have to buy any specialty products – I use my dog's bed! It gives me the same cushiony feeling. (It also teaches him to share.)

You don't have to sit. You can sit or lie down on your bed. I do not recommend lying down – you may fall asleep! I would also check the room temperature. You do not want the room to be too warm. I would keep it on the cooler side. Personally, I like having the ceiling fan on. I enjoy the sound it makes as well as the feeling of air blowing on my face.

This brings me to the next point: distractions. While I like the fan, for you a fan may be a distraction. Nearby clocks, music, and certain scents may be distractions for you. Definitely turn off your phone and other electronics near you.

As time progresses, you will find a space that will work for you. It's nice to have a special spot that makes you feel peaceful. I meditate in the mornings in my bed and in the afternoons on my porch. Sometimes, it's not easy to find a quiet place in a busy household. You need to find the time and place that will work for you. There is no magic about this. Any amount of time that you practice mindfulness is better than none at all. It's a matter of making it a part of your daily routine. You wouldn't skip brushing your teeth – dental health is important. Likewise, don't skip mindfulness – mental health is just as important.

Once you start a mindful exercise, stick with it all of the way through. If you decide on a 20-minute time period and chaos erupts during that 20 minutes, unless there is a fire or a life-threatening emergency, keep up your practice. If you are in a group meditation, the person next to you may snore, sneeze, or pass gas, and this may distract you. These are all common distractions: just bring your awareness back. Here's an extreme example: A friend was teaching a meditation group, and a car came through a wall of the building. She quickly determined that no one was hurt, and so instructed her students to keep meditating.

I prefer to meditate alone in the mornings and with a group in the afternoons when I can. The energy you can get from a group is crazy good! When I was training in Sedona, we meditated in a group setting for 45 minutes. The energy in the room was filled with peacefulness and love. Afterwards, we left to have lunch. When I left the building, all of the colors around me were intensified. I was struck by the beauty of everything around me. I felt blissful. Happy tears were running down my cheeks.

Personally, I don't use music in the background because I am shooting for stillness and quiet, and music interferes with that purpose. But it is an individual choice, and you should do what works for you.

The only necessary piece of equipment when starting a meditation practice is a timer of some kind to keep track of how much time has gone by. There are apps you can get for meditation timers. A popular one is the "Chakra" app.

Meditation and guided mindfulness are different techniques that give similar results. All are geared towards resting your mind. All of us have different preferences.

The terms 'meditation' and 'mindfulness' are often used interchangeably – I know I've done so here. Mindfulness is a form of meditation. There are many forms of meditation, such as contemplation and visualization. All have the common goal of calming our busy minds. The choice will be up to you and what works for you. The following are two methods that I use, and a brief summary on some others. Whatever you choose to do, just know that mindfulness is an investment which requires effort and patience.

SITTING MEDITATION MINDFULNESS

(Mantra)

I use a mantra meditation. Remember, mantras are words that are repeated – they can be a special phrase or other words of significance to you. You can say them aloud or to yourself silently. I was trained to use the method developed by Sarah McLean whereby you use the ancient language of Sanskrit and the subtle sounds of your breath. So while you are meditating, you are focusing not on the meaning of the words, but rather the sound of the words. When you inhale, say to yourself "HAM" (pronounced "hum"). As you exhale, say "SAH.[11]" When I want to use words I understand, I say, "I am clearing." I believe, however, that when you use a mantra, you are connecting with the energy of all of those who have used that mantra before you. Therefore, I don't like to use one that is too obscure.

By using a mantra, we can prevent ourselves from being caught up in a repetitive pattern of thoughts. A mantra helps you to pull yourself into the present. It can create a more positive energy flow. When you find yourself distracted by one of your thoughts, let it go and start repeating your mantra over and over. Remember: mantras are not prayers or affirmations. We are trying to keep away from psychological and emotional levels and focus on vibrational and spiritual levels. When you pick your mantra, it becomes a part of you. You can use it anytime and any place. During my daily activities, if I feel my attention wandering, or an overwhelming emotion threatening to take over, I say my mantra as an anchor to bring me back to my present.

---

11 "Ham sah" is the inverted form of the Sanskrit "Soham" which means "I am he" or "I am that." It is a verbal symbol meaning that you are at one with the universe, or the ultimate reality. This is a common mantra used in Hindu meditation.

You need to find what works for you. What works for me might not work for you, and vice versa. This is a very personal practice.

Consistency is key for rewiring your brain. Studies[12] show that using the same mantra and meditating on a consistent schedule will give you more bang for your buck. Silence is best. Music of any kind can pull your attention outward and distract you.

If you are meditating in the morning, get up, go to the bathroom, and get ready to settle in. Set your timer. Turn off or silence your phone and your laptop, so you aren't tempted by the distraction. If you are a beginner, give yourself 10 – 15 minutes. If possible, do this twice a day.

And so we begin. Follow these steps to start your journey:

- Sit with your spine upright, but relaxed. If you are in a chair, place both feet firmly on the floor. Get comfortable. Try to stay awake and alert – sitting up straight will help this.

- Tuck in your chin and extend your neck to a relaxed position.

- Relax your body as much as you can. Think: where do you keep tension on your body? Begin to release any tension you may feel. Pay attention to your arms, shoulders, and neck. With closed or open eyes, check in with your body and focus your awareness from the inside out, starting from your head all of the way down to your feet and toes. Relax each one so that it is free from tension. Scan your body using the following checklist and note and release any tension you may feel. A ritual scan may also help you sharpen your attention to focus. Check for relaxation in your:

    - Head, scalp, face, mouth eyes, and cheeks;

    - Nose, ears, jaw, and tongue;

    - Neck;

---

12 Deepak Chopra "Quantum Healing: Exploring the Frontiers of Mind/Body Medicine." Bantam Books (1989).

- Shoulders;

- Chest;

- Arms

- Hands;

- Fingers;

- Stomach;

- Back, staring with your upper back, and going down through your middle and lower back;

- Hips, pelvis, and bottom;

- Legs – your thighs, knees, and calves;

- Feet, including each individual toe.

Feel your body in your chair. Do you feel your feet touching the floor? Place your hands on your knees or in your lap. Now do the following:

Close your eyes. Light of any kind can activate your nervous system.

Breathe through your nose. Take four or five slow, deep breaths. Full breaths. Picture your lungs filling up like a balloon. Breathing activates your parasympathetic nervous system, which is in charge of relaxing you. Now breathe naturally, through your nose and without actively controlling your breath. Just observe the sensations of the air going in and out of your body for a few minutes.

Now that you feel relaxed, on your inhale, think of the word "HAM" and on the exhale, think of the word "SAH." Keep focusing on the sensations of your breath while you repeat this pattern: "HAM" "SAH" "HAM" "SAH" "HAM" SAH."

Try to let your mind observe the sounds or the vibrations of the "HAM" and "SAH" as you repeat the mantra. Your attention should be on the sounds of the words, rather than any meaning. Listen to them with EACH breath.

Your thoughts are like waves in the ocean. They flow in and out. When you notice your thoughts drifting in, and you begin to lose your attention, repeat your mantra and breathe again. Refocus your attention.

When your time is up, just sit with your eyes closed for two to three minutes. End your attention on the mantra and your breath. While still in a sitting position, slowly and gently stretch your body. Slowly open your eyes. Don't make any sudden movements or open your eyes right away. It may give you a headache.

If for whatever reason, you do not like the idea of using a mantra, there are alternatives. For example, you can use numbers. Inhale and think "One," exhale and think "Two." Another option is to count your breaths. When you get to 10, start counting backwards. That's a good way to test how mindful you are: if you suddenly find yourself on number 25, you know you slipped into "autopilot." Start all over again until you can focus. Personally, I find the numbers to be distracting, but others find them soothing. Remember: it's all about what works for you!

When I first started to meditate, I kept a meditation journal. I wanted to write about my progression of self-awareness. I also wanted to record how I was feeling both mentally and physically. I did not know a lot of people who meditated, so I was not always sure that what I was feeling was a normal response to the practice. I highly recommend keeping a journal. Even if it is just a few brief sentences scribbled on a calendar, it will motivate you to go back and read your entries and see your progress. It was very difficult at first to stay focused. I experienced what seemed to be endless chatter in my mind. I was going through a great deal of life changes and stressors at the time. I had no idea at first that many of the physical sensations I had noticed were related to that stress.

IMPORTANT TIPS TO REMEMBER

- Many people fall asleep during meditation. Don't worry if you do. Your body will take what it needs from the practice so long as you keep it up. If you are exhausted, you will need sleep. Make sure you do not meditate after a full meal – that's a guaranteed path towards falling asleep during meditation! I once went to a lecture given by Deepak Chopra. Someone asked what it meant that he kept falling asleep during meditation. Deepak replied, "It means you are tired and need sleep."

- Everyone experiences sensations and physical movements during meditation. Just think of all the stress and tension your body has pent up inside. There are going to be physical sensations and involuntary movements as it releases. Trust me – I noticed everything at first. My foot fell asleep. My leg twitched. I had ringing in my ears. I saw colors of pink and blue, and my toes were cold. All of this was normal. Your mind and body are resting and relaxing – these are only signs that the stress is releasing. Some people even feel like they are tilting off their axis.

- Most people report having a 'beginner's nod.' Have you ever been sitting up while you are tired, and your head starts to tilt forwards when you start to fall asleep? This is similar. The only difference is that you will still hear the sounds around you and you have not fallen asleep at all. You have merely gone father into yourself. Suddenly, you will realize the time has flown by. Instead of thinking you have acres of more time ahead, you are nearly finished!

- You may notice tears streaming down your face, or a joyful, blissful feeling that you have not felt before. If you do, congratulations! This is a sure sign you are doing it correctly.

Here's another method you can try using nothing but your breath. Breathing is a natural way our body is able to relax. It is free and can be used anywhere at any time!

THE MINDFULNESS OF BREATHING

- Set your timer for 10-15 minutes.
- Sit in a chair or on a cushion. Make sure that you are comfortable and the temperature in the room is adjusted for your comfort. Put your feet firmly on the floor. Find your balance.
- Make sure your back is straight in the chair.
- Relax your body.
- Place your hands in your lap or on your knees.
- Close your eyes.
- Feel your body in the chair, your back against the chair, the weight of your bottom and your thighs on the chair.
- Check into your body. Pay attention to the specific parts of your body that are stressed and tense. Roll your neck and shoulders up and down a few times.
- Notice how your feet feel on the floor.
- Soften your eyes.
- Soften your cheeks.
- Soften your jaw.
- Soften your mouth.

- Soften your face.

- Soften your shoulders.

- Soften your neck.

- Soften your chest.

- Soften your belly.

- Soften your pelvis.

- Breathe in, taking a deep breath. Slowly exhale through your nose. Do this five times in a row.

- Notice your body and how you are breathing. See if you can feel the breath in your body. Notice the rise and fall of your belly as it expands and contracts with each breath.

- Notice your chest rise and fall as you breathe.

- Breathe normally. Inhale, then exhale. Repeat those words to yourself as you breathe: "Inhale, then exhale." Notice the coolness of the air on your inhale, and the warmth of the air on your exhale.

- Make sure your observations of the sensations and movements of your breaths are natural and effortless. This should be relaxing. Don't feel the need to control or manipulate your breathing. It's like observing the air from an oscillating fan as it goes back and forth across your face. You don't control the air. It is a neutral state of observation. No conscious thoughts. You may notice that your breathing patterns change. They may be faster, slower, shallower, or deeper. This is normal. You are just more aware.

- As your thoughts start to flow in your mind like passing clouds on a sunny day, use your breath as an anchor to manage your mind and stay focused.

- Distractions are common. Notice them, release them, and gently go back to your inhale, then exhale.

- Remember: with each breath you are releasing stress.

- After your time is up, sit with your eyes closed for a few minutes and take your attention gradually off of your breathing. Slowly open your eyes and begin to move around.

A regular practice of mindfulness exercises like these produces many beneficial qualities. You will find that you have enhanced clarity of thought, creativeness, and focus. The more you are able to stay in your present, the less impact negative events will have on you. Your immune system will strengthen. If you have surgery, your post-surgical relief will be accelerated: you will have less pain, and your emotional response will be better.

Here are some other benefits you will receive from regular practice of these exercises:

- Increased activation of your left PFC (prefrontal cortex) which helps you control and reduce sadness, depression, and other negative emotions.

- Added neural connections to your insula[13] and increases gray matter. This will increase your self-awareness, compassion, and empathy towards others.

- Thickening of the cortical layers in the attention areas of your brain – this will let you pay better attention!

- Reduced anxiety due to the increased activity in the ventromedial prefrontal cortex, the area that controls worrying. It also increases the activity in the anterior cingulate cortex, the governing area of thinking and our emotions.

- Reduced stress and cortisol levels.

- Improved emotional intelligence.

---

13 The insula is a radically underappreciated part of the brain. It's been called by Daniel Siegel, M.D., "the information superhighway" that runs up and down between higher, cortical brain areas, lower, limbic areas, and the body.

- Strengthened areas of your brain that lift your mood and increase your ability to learn.

- Increased and improved working memory, impulsivity, and reaction speeds.

- Enhanced physical stamina and resilience.

- Reduced addictive and self-destructive behaviors.

- Reduced aging at the cellular level.

- Improved control of blood sugar.

- Improved heart and circulatory health via lowered blood pressure.

- Lessened fear and loneliness.

- Increased relaxing optimism.

- Prevention of emotional eating and nervous behaviors such as smoking.

- Enhanced self-esteem and self-acceptance.

- Increased mental strength and focus, giving you a leg up on ignoring distractions.

- Increased creativity and productivity.

- Less multitasking.

- Decreased inflammatory disorders and cellular-level inflammation; reduction in PMS and menopausal symptoms; reduced Alzheimer's risk; better-managed heart rate; and reduction in the rate of stroke.

- Better decision-making and problem-solving skills.

- Increased memory retention and recall.

- Better connections to your world, increasing positive social connections.

****

These are just a few examples of my personal practice that I include in my daily life. I started out meditating twice a day for 10 minutes. I gradually increased my time. I enjoy the time that I have with myself, and I wish that I could meditate all day! But, that's not realistic. After years of practice, I meditate every morning for 30 minutes, around 20 minutes in the afternoon on weekdays, and I have a guided meditation[14] at night before bed. On the weekends, I meditate for 45 minutes on Sundays and when I can on Saturdays. This schedule is not set in stone – believe me! Sometimes I can only find 10 or 15 minutes here or there, or I might do a few mindfulness exercises and focus on open awareness. We will talk more about open awareness in the next chapter.

---

14 A guided meditation is a form of meditation which has evolved more recently. In these meditations, either live or via a recording, you are given out loud, step-by-step instructions through a meditative experience.

CHAPTER SIX

MIND TOOLS 2.0

"There are many good forms of meditation practice. A good meditation practice is any one that develops awareness or mindfulness of our body and our sense, of our mind and heart."
~Jack Kornfield

Rather than just give you instructions on some mindfulness exercises, I thought it might be helpful if you knew *how* these exercises would be helpful, and *why* they work. In my experience, people tend to stick to something more when they understand why they are doing it. I've also included examples of how these practices helped me. These exercises may appeal to you more than formal meditation, and you may find ways to fit them into your busy schedule. It doesn't matter what you do – so long as you do it!

Think back to the most stressful time in your life. It may be happening this very minute. For me, and, I would think, most of us, there are many stressful times to choose from. One such time that comes to my mind was years ago. My husband was working on a business deal that would bring in a large commission. That payout would have taken a great deal of stress off of all of us. He worked for many months and countless hours trying to make this happen. At times, I ignored my gut – I had a feeling this would not come through. He had people connected to the project call me to reassure me. All would be ok. So much of our life was dependent upon this deal going through. The day of the wire transfer, we were visiting my parents. We were lined up to celebrate. All day I kept worrying – I was thinking about past projects that had fallen through. What would I do if this fell through? I worried about moving again and how the kids would take the news. I was frustrated and angry. I was on edge all morning. I was overwhelmed, and my mind shifted back and forth between anxiety and excitement. I was a wreck.

Later in the day, the wire did not come. The organizer of the financing was a fraud and took all the money and disappeared. I became unhinged. I yelled and wasn't thinking at all about what I was saying. I was pure reaction. My thoughts were solely on the future and the what-ifs and what-nows. Back then, I didn't have any tools in my tool belt to pull myself back up and into the moment.

I know that there are so many people today that understand this feeling of emotional depletion and are clueless how to pull themselves back up. Instead, we tend to focus on the endless negative chatter in our heads that are on an endless automatic replay loop. Sometimes we allow our anxieties and fears to shake and control our inner core. We feel stuck and immobilized.

I can tell you from my own experience that I was able to ultimately retrieve my mind. I am happy now. It took motivation, soul searching, time, practice, and patience on many levels. I was very lucky to have the opportunity, even though I didn't recognize it at the time, to lock myself away from everyone and focus on mindfulness. I read countless books and viewed more Ted Talks and YouTube videos than I can remember. I enrolled in the McLean Meditation Institute lead by Sarah McLean. I know now how fortunate I was to have the kind of life that allowed me to do this. Keep in mind that even if you can't fully immerse yourself because of your daily obligations, even a half hour a day will have a lasting effect. I can tell you from personal experience and without a doubt that mindfulness is a daily practice that allows you to slowly build an acceptance to the things in life that you cannot change. You can rewire your brain for acceptance. You will be more focused and in the present. You will be aware of the here and now without focusing on "how" the here and now is happening. The more I practiced mindfulness, the more I was aware of my thoughts and feelings as I experienced them.

I started my days with a guided imagery, in which I am taken by a meditation guide through a series of relaxing visualizations. I scanned my body for tension and anxiety. Believe it or not, the mere acknowledgment of being overwhelmed and anxious can lessen the feelings of being overwhelmed and anxious. I was committed to refusing to allow my negative thinking to take over my mind or my emotions. When I started to think, "I will never be able to start over again!" I very quickly tried to replace that thought with a positive one. I reminded myself to focus on the present. This constant reminder of staying in the present kept me from focusing on the how and why the present was happening. My frame of mind was positive for longer periods of time each day.

Through mindful activities and focusing on the present I stopped thinking about the "shoulds," how things were supposed to be, and my visions of how my life needed to be. I was very aware of my brain's natural default position: thinking about the past and future rather than the now.

I needed to find some control in my life, and mindfulness was an answer. I had the power to find my "center." I reminded myself of this often. No matter how good or bad your life has been, our intrinsic wholeness is always present, and we can see it if we go looking for it. Everything on this Earth is connected, wherever you are, and whatever you are doing. You can start accepting your life as it is without making judgments. If I can do it – so can you! It's not easy. It's a new pattern you are developing in your newly rewired brain. But, if you are tired of being tired, this is a great start. Fear of the future will only block you and increase those negative thoughts.

I want to stop here to point out that none of this means you need to be blind to reality. Some things are just inarguably bad – like if someone you love is dying. The 'trick' is not to avoid your feelings about what is happening, but to experience it fully. While you are holding your mother's hand on her deathbed, focus on her hand. Is her hand warm or cold? Is her skin dry or moist? Don't judge the moment, just fully immerse yourself in it. For example, don't say to yourself, "this is the worst day of my life." Say to yourself, "I am with my mother, and I am easing her transition. I am looking into her face and fully present for her."

I am a visual person, so when I was learning how to "center" myself, I wanted to picture something. My center is in the middle of my chest, and it is filled with water. Bruce Lee is often quoted as saying, "Be like water." I need to be around water. It flows, it's calming, it sometimes sparkles: it's mesmerizing. Water is often used as a metaphor for different emotions. The water in my center represents my emotional state. On the surface, it can be calm, wavy, deep, or shallow, or it can crash into the coastline and be volatile. But, no matter what is happening above, the water underneath at the bottom is calm and still.

So, when I sense that I am starting to feel stressed out, I use centering breaths as a tool to guide me back to my present. I put my hand on my chest to feel my center and the water inside.

Deeply inhale.

Fill your lungs for six seconds – hold the air in your lungs for five seconds.

Exhale slowly and gradually, releasing your breath over seven seconds.

Repeat this four or five times.

Stay with your breath.

Visualizing that space in your chest will also help you to visualize the space in between what is happening in this exact moment and your response to what is happening. That centering breath will give your nervous system a moment to kick in and bring your thoughts and feelings to the surface, without judgment. And, with a level of calmness, you make the decision how to respond or react.

This is an exercise that you need to practice over and over. You need to step away from yourself and evaluate your progress. Are you more reactive or responsive? Do you have a tendency to allow that negative bias to enter your thoughts, or do you take the time to find your center and take a deep breath first? Just remember, if you allow your emotions to take over, you are not seeing the big picture. Those emotionally-based responses are not always – or even usually – the most creative or productive. When I am making big decisions in my life, I have a 24-hour rule. This gives me plenty of time to rest my brain and stay in my center. The stillness allows me room to connect with my gut feelings. People around you may want an immediate response, but you have to think of yourself and put yourself first. How many times in the past did you immediately react and then regret your decision?

Over time, you can employ what the Buddhists describe as a "Watcher" over your sacred center space. The Watcher is inside the water in your Center. When something happens in your life, the Watcher sets off an alert. "A wave is coming! Let's breathe first!" The Watcher is your conscious, helping you to stay calm, slow down, and flow with the water.

Dr. Martin Seligman, a "positive psychologist," says that whether you are using meditation mindfulness or other mindfulness activities, you will be in a state of "flow" when you are lost in creating. When you are in stillness, nothing matters, nothing exists, except what you are doing at that moment. Because you are so engrossed in the process of what you are doing, time stops. You lose your sense of self. You concentrate on the present and have deep, effortless involvement. In this state, you may experience the following blissful states:

- You may forget yourself, let go, and let be.

- You have no worries, thoughts, or anxiety. They have all melted away.

- You feel a oneness with the world.

- Your whole being becomes absorbed in this state.

- You use all of your senses and *don't think* about how you are feeling.

When I meditate, I feel like I am floating in the middle of nowhere. It's spontaneous, and it can't be forced. I am sitting down, and I am absorbed totally in the activity. My whole body is involved in working towards stillness.

My quest to become the Most Knowledgeable Mindfulness Trainer on the Planet began during the summer that I was enrolled in the program with Sarah McLean. I loved meditation and the breathing exercises, but I was determined to get a better understanding of mindfulness and why it worked. Sarah assigned one of my favorite mindfulness exercises. It really introduces the concept of a "Beginner's Mind."

Each time I dined out during a two-week period, I instructed the waitress to ask the chef to prepare whatever he wanted for my meal. Please note that I was new in St. Michaels, a very small harbor town on the Chesapeake Bay in Maryland. It isn't commonplace for someone to make such a request, especially during the busy summer season. There are only four restaurants in St. Michaels, and I made this odd request in all four of them. I was pleasantly surprised to find that they were all very excited to participate in my practice. Each night I was gleeful as I set about mindfully exploring my meal. I entered each night with an open mind, ready to redirect my attention on each morsel without any preconceived notions.

Each night I felt like a kid at Christmas. There were no judgments or prejudices. It was like waiting to open a package using all five of my senses. There were no expectations. Each night I stayed in my present for 10 to 15 minutes, feeling the texture of the food, looking at it, smelling it, tasting it, hearing the satisfying crunches and slurps it made. I fully engaged my attention on what I was eating. I explored these meals that were made with love and kindness simply for me to enjoy. I took it all in, alone in my own reverie. I observed the dish the meal came in. I saw the colors and textures, sizes and shapes before me. I smelled the food and noted its location. I touched the food with my fingers and my mouth, exploring how it felt in my mouth as well as how it tasted. I listened to myself chewing and felt the sensations as the food slid down my throat into my stomach. I was focused on this meal only for the entire time, not thinking of anything else. If a stray thought wandered into my mind, I quickly banished it and circled back to the present. I was not thinking about whether I liked or disliked the food. I was just experiencing the food, enjoying each and every bite. I challenge you to try this. When you are concentrating on the food in front of you, you have less room for chatter in your head.

Before I give you a list of other mindfulness exercises to try, I want to introduce a new concept for some of you. It's called "disconnect."

Throughout my meditation training, I picked a day – Wednesday – and christened it "True Solitude Wednesdays." On those days, I turned off all of my electronics. I started off slowly, easing into the silence. First two hours, then three, then eventually the entire day. I unplugged myself from the world. No phone, music, television, computers, or even speech. Just me.

At the time, I lived alone in the middle of nowhere, which made this easier. Nonetheless, I would call my mother and my children and tell them I would be off the grid and unable to be reached for the next eight hours. I made sure that I had food and other supplies I might need.

This kind of aloneness and inner focus was both inspiring and daunting. I found every excuse known to man to call or speak to someone. The first few times I tried it, I prayed for a mail delivery, just so I could speak to another human being, however briefly. I took long walks, meditated, and prayed. I took a 30-minute bath. I mindfully cleaned and cooked and ate foods. I avoided activities that took attention from myself. Since that time, I have gone on a three-day silent retreat, and I am looking forward to a planned 10-day silent retreat this coming fall.

No pressure, no judgments.

Expand your boundaries.

Try something new.

Not everyone will be able to dedicate an entire day to rest their minds.

Any amount of time will help and will be worthwhile.

A Time Mobility poll in 2012 reported that 84% of cell phone users could not go a full day without usage. We don't realize our level of addiction to our technology until we observe how strong the pull is when we don't have them. It can be a bit of a shock to your system, taking away its tiny but constant hits of dopamine, but honestly, it is a healing experience. To this day, I really prefer at least a half-day of silence and taking a mindful walk or bike ride. I rediscovered my mind and my gut from this stillness. I have grown and evolved. I also rejuvenated my nervous system.

Shutting off the electronics and having time alone to yourself can be a wake-up call. I could not believe how out of touch with myself I was. It was so quiet that I was not sure what to do first. I found hundreds, if not thousands, of distractions. Given that we live a life amid constant stimulation, this is not surprising. You may also find that you feel twitches and small pains. The important thing here is to avoid getting caught up in these little distractions and float away with them.

You will encounter many thoughts along the way. You will have frequent visits from those negative recordings tempting your fears and anxieties. Cutting yourself off from your world, you may feel as if you are missing out on something important, or being left out socially. Dismiss these fears: no matter if you take 30 minutes or four hours or one week off, stillness will be something you want more of once you are able to achieve it. Find a balance that works for you.

Silence is a means by which you can learn more about yourself and who you are. In silence, you can evaluate and reflect. It just takes time to reconnect to that person you see in the mirror every day. Once you start a consistent practice of Disconnect, you will objectively observe how much time we live our lives caught in the moment of a perceived urgency. Most things that seem urgent aren't really when you take the time to examine them. This isn't to say that all of your problems will suddenly disappear, but you will re-energize your sense of purpose. Free from distractions and things to do that stand in the way of your purpose, you will be in for an interesting journey.

Mindfulness is a natural process. You may not be aware of it, but you may already include some mindfulness practices in your day to day life. Stop and think of any activity you do where you feel as it nothing exists but what you are doing. Time stops, and you lose all sense of self. I do this in my Pilates class, and also when I run. Sometimes I think about my great-grandmother. I don't have a lot of clear memories of her except this one: sitting in her room praying on her rosary. She was totally immersed in what she was doing – her present. The problem for us is that we are mindful only for brief periods of time. Most likely only seconds. We need to practice having more mindfulness periods and making those periods more lengthy and deep.

Try this one:

BURNING CANDLE MEDITATION
(Practiced by gazing at a candle)

This exercise requires a prepared space. It's best not to be in a brightly lit room. Before you begin, close the shades and turn down the lights. Light a candle, and place it on a small table three to four feet in front of you. Now that you have set the stage, do the following:

- Sit in a comfortable posture with the spine upright, and the arms and shoulders relaxed. You can assume any meditative posture which you can maintain without any movement for the duration of this meditation time. This should be a position that feels comfortable and right for you. Use a chair, or sit on the floor.

- Make sure that the flame is at the level of your eyes. Face the candle directly so that you don't have to turn your neck at all to see it.

- Take a few deep breaths to relax. Close your eyes and observe your breath as you inhale and exhale for about five to seven breaths. This will allow your breath to settle down and help bring you into the present moment.

- Open your eyes, and gaze at the flame intently and keep your eyes on it.

- Keep your vision focused and steady on the flame without blinking for as long as it is comfortable to you. Make sure you are looking at the flame, not the candle itself or the wick.

- Try to maintain your awareness and focus on the flame.

- Try to resist the urge to move around. Be still.

- As you go deeper into this type of meditation, staring at the light of the flame interrupts the signals that are sent from the optic nerves to your eyes. This affects your peripheral vision. Gradually, you will be less and less aware of what you can see to your sides, and you will be more and more focused on what is in front of you – the flame.

- Try to allow any thoughts to flow away from you like a cloud. Stray thoughts are to be expected – don't beat yourself up when they arrive!

- Imagine that you are breathing the light of the candle in and out of yourself with each breath.

- Continue to gaze at the flame until you cannot keep your eyes open and tears start flowing. Once this happens, close your eyes.

- When you close your eyes, you may be able to visualize an after-image of the flame with your closed eyes. Focus on this after-image as long as it exists.

WALKING MINDFULNESS EXERCISE

There are many types of walking mindfulness. You can choose a short walk up and down hallways at work, or a long walk outside. Either experience will help you become present and connect to what is happening in the here and how.

This is something that was hard for me at first because I used to take long walks in order to find clarity in my thoughts. I used these times to ponder over my issues. During this exercise, however, *we do not think*. You will be directing your mind in a different way. Also, walking will bring energy to your brain. If you are walking outside, make sure you are wearing comfortable clothing and shoes. Give yourself a set time of 15-20 minutes.

- Begin by taking three deep breaths through your nose. Inhale and exhale slowly. Then notice your awareness of your body and how it feels.

- Take a few seconds and answer these questions. Think about them – don't feel pressure to give rushed answers. How does your body feel when you walk? Is it light or heavy? Is it relaxed or stiff? Be aware of your posture. Are you straight or slightly bent over? Do you lean to one side?

- Try not to be self-conscious, but begin some self-awareness and notice how you walk. Is your step heavy or light? Is your stride long or short? Do you favor one leg over another? Don't change anything, just observe.

- Feel the weight of your body pressing down toward the ground and your heels pushing into your shoes. Become aware of all the subtle movements that are keeping you balanced and upright.

- Allow your knees to bend very slightly and feel your hips as your center of gravity. Take a few deep belly breaths, and bring your awareness into the present moment.

LOST, FOUND & REWIRED   91

- Begin to walk at a slightly slower than normal pace. Keep an almost imperceptible bend in your knees. With each step, be aware of the gentle heel-to-toe rhythm as each foot makes contact with the ground.

- Breathe naturally and fully, filling your lungs to capacity with each inhalation, but not so much that you strain or struggle in any way.

- Allow your eyes to focus softly ahead of you, taking in as much of the periphery as you are comfortable doing. Try to maintain a soft body and breathing awareness as you walk naturally and easily.

- When your attention drifts away from the sensations of walking and breathing, take notice of those thoughts, moods, or emotions without judgment and gently guide your awareness back to the present moment, back to the walking.

- Observe what is going on around you – other people, cars, signs, trees, and the ground under your feet.

- What colors or shapes are around you? Are there movements like wind or trees blowing? Notice any cars driving by. Is there water nearby? Notice stillness. You are not thinking about what you are looking at, merely observing it.

- Pay attention to the sounds. What do you hear as it is coming into your awareness? Take a minute and close your eyes and just listen to sounds.

- Turn your attention to smells. Are they nice or unpleasant? If you pick up a smell, try not to attach a story or association with it. Sometimes smells can remind us of a person or occasion. My mind always seems to turn to food. Be careful this doesn't distract you – for example, a smell will make me think of an ingredient in pizza, and then who has the best pizza, and so on.

- Notice physical sensations and feelings during your walk. Is there a breeze? What is the temperature? Cool or warm? Can you feel the sun on your skin? How does it feel? What about your legs and feet? How do they feel as they touch the ground with each step? How about your arms? How do they feel? What are they doing? Are they by your side or in a bent position? Do they swing as you walk? Just notice the sensations and not any feelings attached to those sensations. Don't create a story about why your big toe is painful inside of your shoe because of that darn shopping cart that ran over your foot. Just notice how your big toe feels.

- Allow your thoughts to come and go without lingering. Thoughts will appear and then be replaced by the next thing you see, feel, or notice.

- Start to notice the sensations of the movement of your body. The way it feels when the soles of your feet touch the ground. From your right side to your left. Shift your weight from side to side and then back again.

- Pay attention to the pace of your walk and your rhythm. Try not to change it – though that is a natural reaction. I remember the first time I noticed I was waddling when I was pregnant – I did my best to change that gait immediately! But the purpose of this exercise is not change – it is awareness.

- Notice your reactions as you walk. If a car beeps at you as you walk through the crosswalk, were you frustrated or impatient? What happens when someone in front of you suddenly stops as they seem to always do at Costco on a Saturday? How are you feeling as you get closer to your goal?

When the walking meditation is over, allow yourself to come to a gentle stop. Pause for a moment, once again noticing what it is like to stand still and feel the Earth solid beneath your feet. Take a few deep breaths as this session ends. Slowly return to your regular activity.

MINDFULNESS WALKING AT WORK

Sometimes you can't walk outdoors. The weather may make it prohibitive, or you simply can't remove yourself from the location you are in. It may be easier for you to take a break in a stressful day by walking in the hallways at work rather than explaining why you have to leave work for a little while.

If you can, find a quiet hallway or room. Take off your shoes, if possible. Find a place where you can walk for at least 12-14 steps before you have to turn around.

- First, notice your body as you stand in stillness. Feel the connection of your body to the ground or the floor. Become aware of your surroundings, taking in any sights, smells, tastes, sounds, or other sensations. Notice any thoughts or emotions. When you find them, let them go. Notice your arms by your side, or hold your right hand in your left hand at the front or, if you prefer, clasp your hands at the small of your back. Notice your breath coming in and out of your body. Breathe normally. Just let it be.

- As you begin to walk, your primary focus is on the sensations of walking.

- Allow your awareness to focus on the sense of stepping on the ground. Lift your knees a little bit higher than you normally would, and decrease your stride so that you are taking shorter steps. Notice how it feels to step on the Earth. Stepping, stepping, stepping.

- Now slow down enough so that you notice the mechanics of lifting your foot and then placing it back down on the ground. Lifting, stepping, lifting, stepping, lifting stepping.

- Notice when your mind wanders, and don't worry about it. Just keep bringing it back to the sensations of lifting and stepping, and to the awareness of that sequence.

- Slow down a little bit more, and notice the shift in your weight. Lifting, stepping, shifting, lifting, stepping, shifting, lifting, stepping, shifting.

- Now shift your weight to your left leg and begin to lift your right foot. Move your right foot forwards and put it back down on the ground. Mindfully shift your weight to your right leg, and begin to lift up your left food, move it forward, and put it back down on the ground.

- Continue with this walking. Walking mindfully, slowly, and paying attention to the soles of your feet. As each part of the sole, from heel to toe, touches the ground, be aware of the sensations. Lifting, moving, placing, lifting, moving, placing. Notice how your body moves as you walk. Try to walk with awareness. One step at a time.

- When it is time to turn, maintain the flow of mindfulness and bring your awareness to the intricate process of turning around. Slowly, and with attention to each movement necessary to turn, begin to walk back to where you began. One step at a time. Lifting, moving, shifting, stepping, placing, lifting, moving, shifting, stepping, placing. You will find a rhythm that works for you. Everyone's center of balance and body is different.

- When you move forward, feel your whole body. Feel your head sitting on your shoulders, your arms and hands, your belly, your legs, and your core, all moving you forward, step by step.

- Notice any thoughts that arise and let them alone. Just go back to your focus on the sensation of walking. Lifting, moving, shifting, stepping, placing. Notice your breath. Has it moved into a pattern? A rhythm that fits with the pace of your walking, step by step? Notice your breath, but don't change your breathing consciously.

- The next time you return to your starting place, stand quietly. Notice the sensations in your body and what is going on with your breath. Be aware of the stillness when the movement stops. Be happy for the time you have spent today, practicing the mindfulness of walking.

If you are easily distracted or bored, this exercise may be difficult for you. If this is the case, try counting and walking. Walk at a normal pace. When you take your first step, count "one." On the next two steps you say, "one, two." On the next three steps you say, "one, two, three." And so on all the way up until 10. When you reach ten, then reverse the process – start with "ten" and then "ten, nine" and then "ten, nine, eight" and so on. If you find that you have lost count, just start again with one.

EVERY DAY MINDFULNESS EXERCISES

There are a number of things you can do to keep yourself mindful during your regular everyday activities. Here are just a few of them:

- If you jog or do other regular exercise, you can incorporate this into your practice as well. Feel the general movement of the body, and in particular, the rhythm of the feet on the ground.

- Moving the body in intentional forms such as yoga or from our own internal sense of rhythm can very much be a part of our cultivation of mindfulness.

- Throughout the day, take a few moments to bring your attention to your breath. It's a fast way to bring a calm and clear state of mind. Take five mindful breaths. Inhale and exhale completely. Focus on your breath entering and exiting your body. Let go of any thoughts.

- Use the sound of a bell as a way to remind you of your mindfulness. Whenever you hear a bell, a phone, a car horn, or a train whistle, let it be a signal to you to listen and be in your present.

- Relax, Remember, Release, and Return. When you are distracted by a thought, sensation or sound, check and see if it brings tension to your body. If so, try your best to release that tension. RELAX. Recognize that you were distracted. REMEMBER that simply being aware of being distracted is, in fact, mindful. RELEASE the distraction and place your focus on your breath. RETURN once you have released the distraction and relax and breathe. You will find yourself with a fresh focus and awareness.

MINDFULNESS EATING EXERCISE

Here is a ten-minute meditation designed to help you practice mindful eating. This exercise is an amusing practice that allows you to focus on the tastes, sensations, and textures of the food you are eating in order to bring yourself back to the present. It is one of my favorite exercises because it involves food – duh! You are going to use as many of your senses as you can, not just taste and smell.

Before you begin, pick a small piece of food. It can be a cookie, piece of fruit, chocolate, slice of cheese, or whatever you want. It should be something you can eat in two bites.

- Pick up a small piece of the food.

- Do you feel anticipation? Do you feel an urge to eat the food quickly? What are your emotions?

- Look at the food. Notice its texture. What color is it? How much does it weigh?

- Close your eyes, and explore the food with the sense of touch. What does it feel like? It is hard? Soft? Sticky? Grainy? Moist? Dry?

- Before you eat it, explore your sense of smell. What do you notice? Does it trigger any of your other senses?

- Take your first bite. Chew slowly. Don't think about the food, just be aware of the sensory experience of chewing and tasting. Close your eyes and focus.

- Notice how the food's texture feels in your mouth. What is its consistency?

- Are there any flavor changes? Are they moment to moment?

- Move the food around your mouth. Notice what is happening to your mouth, lips, teeth, and tongue.

- Slowly finish your bite of food. Be as mindful as you can.

- Now, take your second and last bite.

- As before, chew very slowly while paying close attention to the actual sensory experience of eating. Be aware of the sensations and movements of chewing, the flavor of the food as it changes, and the sensations of swallowing.

- Enjoy trying to focus your attention, moment by moment.

- Is there any lingering taste after you have swallowed?

- Now that you are finished, how do you feel?

BODY SCAN MEDITATION

A body scan can take between 10 and 20 minutes. You can scan your body in a chair or lie down. Get comfortable and warm. Take five mindful breaths.

- Check in with your body just as it is right now. Notice the sensations that are present, feeling the contact your body is making with the floor.

- Start at the crown of the head, noticing any sensations you may feel. Is there tingling? Numbness? Tightness? Relaxation? Move to include the rest of your head and forehead. Notice whether or not you can feel the pulse in your forehead, or whether there is tightness or ease.

- Feel your face. Notice your jaw, the sensations in your mouth, including the roof of your mouth and your tongue. Soften your eyes, your right cheek, and your left cheek.

- Feel your nose, the right and left nostril separately. Feel the breath passing through both nostrils. Is the air cool or warm?

- Bring your awareness to your ears, how they feel, and whether they are hearing or receiving sounds.

- Feel your throat and neck, and be aware of any tension in your neck and throat.

- Move down to your right shoulder, right arm, elbow, forearm, wrist, hand, thumb, and each of your individual fingers.

- Move down to your left shoulder, left arm, elbow, forearm, wrist, hand, thumb, and each of your individual fingers.

- Feel your chest. Notice the smooth rise and fall of the chest. Inhale and exhale slowly. Turn your awareness to your ribcage, side ribs, and your upper and lower back. Feel the sensations of your back against your chair. Become aware of your entire back.

- Turn your awareness to your belly and move your awareness to the pelvic area. Feel the weight of your legs, the right hip and the right thigh, the right knee, calf, ankle, the top of the foot, the sole of the foot, the right big toe and all of the individual toes. Feel your entire foot, notice and release sensations or tensions.

- Now move to your left hip. Examine the left thigh, the left knee, calf, ankle, the top of the foot, the sole of the foot, the left big toe and all of the individual toes. Feel your entire foot, notice and release sensations or tensions.

- Take two deep breaths. Feel the energy flowing all over your body.

CHAPTER SEVEN

SHIFT HAPPENS

*"You have the choice to let go of whatever you have been holding onto...
including an old identity that no longer serves you...Be authentic is a
moment to moment proposition, a never ending journey...Honor the space
between no longer and not yet."*
~Nancy Levin

The practice of meditation was in my life for many years. However, it was also somewhat inconsistent. I did not consciously internalize the benefits of mindfulness and how it could help transition me through the rough and challenging aspects of my life.

Several years ago, I thought I was in a great place. I was in a great relationship, and my kids were both college bound. However, I felt an inner restlessness and the need to re-evaluate my life. I was feeling like I was running on empty on an emotional level. I decided to take the board exam for life coaching and also work towards my certification to become a meditation teacher. As a therapist, I was aware of transitional periods in a person's life. It can be much harder to apply what you know in your own life when it seems so obvious in other people's lives. It's hard to get perspective from the inside.

I was clueless as to how this mindfulness practice would have such a significant impact on my life. Please know that everyone's journey will be different. So, as I describe mine, please keep in mind that you shouldn't expect the same thing. Also, please DO NOT make major life decisions like relationship or job changes during this process. Just stay in your present.

During my mindfulness training, I prepared daily with readings, journal entries, and (obviously) meditation and mindfulness exercises. At the same time, I was writing the chapter for "Miami Breast Cancer Experts[15]" on mindfulness and breast cancer. All of these tasks required a distraction free environment. For me, living with my family and four dogs made for a difficult environment in which to accomplish anything. My significant other had worked very hard and was lucky enough to retire relatively young. We spent most of our days together.

I believe Carlos was proud of my desires, yet he also wanted to be the center of my world. In order to be distraction-free to accomplish what I needed to do, I left and headed to the Eastern Shore of Maryland. It was quiet, peaceful, rustic, and so quiet I'll say "quiet" again. No one called my name 15 times a day. I had peace and quiet in which to think, write, meditate, and do something for myself. This was a task that was foreign to me. I remember one Sunday I stayed in bed the entire day. I read, ate, and wrote. I discovered Netflix. While I was there, I gave myself permission to have my "True Solitude Wednesdays." I discovered that I loved silence I felt that I was re-introducing myself to the person I saw in the mirror every day. Each morning and every afternoon, I meditated for 30 minutes. I was relaxed, peaceful, and excited to share my self-reflections. A new and improved me was emerging.

I seemed to start isolating myself without recognizing that was what I was doing. I was oversensitive to people and sounds. I avoided conflict, drama, and negative interactions at all costs. I was sad. On the one hand, I was more responsive and less reactive to situations of conflict, yet at the same time, I felt intolerant of some of the people that I interacted with on a regular basis. The people around me were happier with the old me.

I began to feel as though I was growing and self-actualizing and as a result, I felt like I was not fitting into my surroundings the way I once did. I wanted to expand my relationship with Carlos. I wanted to meditate,

---

15 "Miami Breast Cancer Experts" by Cindy Papale-Hammontree and Sabrina Hernandez-Cano (2015).

eat healthy foods, move away from toxic relationships and try to open ourselves to new experiences and people. Carlos preferred dining with the same people, on the same night, at the same restaurant. He preferred the old routine. Our life was good in so many ways. But his 'normal' was not my 'normal' and vice versa. I was frustrated trying to explain my need for change. He was frustrated that I was transforming in front of his very eyes. We lived a very 'Miami' lifestyle of drinking and dining. Our communication was breaking down. Excessive drinking and other toxic behaviors like temper tantrums, threats, and sexual inappropriateness increased.

I felt the need to pull him away to the Eastern Shore where I had found such peace and tranquility. I wanted us to heal and repair our relationship. He agreed. I was relieved! But, in the end, he did not come and meet me. Two weeks later, he drove cross-country with his son, and he reconnected with a former girlfriend. Pretty bad, right? I spent that summer working on mediation training. The best thing for my soul and my broken heart.

Here is something important to note: in hindsight, Carlos felt betrayed and angry. It took me a long time to understand this point of view. In a way, I did betray him. He fell in love with the woman that I was – a loving, selfless caretaker. For years I lived contentedly in a predictable environment. That's what he signed up for. I'm the one who changed the game plan. All the while I was growing, stretching and transforming, and he did not want to give me the space to grow. He thrived on sameness and predictability. He wanted routine. It made him happy and calm. When I played along, I made him happy. When I changed, he was unhappy, and he wanted to hurt me as much as he could so that we would both feel as deeply unhappy as he did. In the end, neither I nor his ex-girlfriend ended up with him.

What is the point of disclosing these personal details? Meditation and mindfulness did not ruin my relationship or give me the tools to save it. But it did cause the shifts in my personality, the physical and emotional changes, that were ultimately the downfall of our relationship. The point is this: change will happen, ultimately for the better, but it is change. I was unaware of my shifting and purification period as I was going through it, and you may not either. Therefore, it is important that you share your journey with your significant other. Discuss it with your partner, and your meditation teacher. A trained professional should be able to guide you through these changes in a way which will be the least disruptful of your life. Unless, of course, your life needs disrupting. Just be prepared. I wasn't, and I will never know whether or not this would have made a difference in my life.

Don't be afraid that if you start a meditation practice, you will somehow lose control and magically begin a new life. You are not under any pressure to start a new life, or make changes, and most people find that the changes are subtler than what I went through.

And whatever changes occur are unlikely to be sudden. Your gradual development of a quiet and clear awareness will bring changes in your life naturally. At some point, you may re-evaluate and start to clean up your life in some manner. You may pull back from those things or people that seem to be holding you back from your desire to stay positive and in the present. Diversions in your life that pulled you before may now be replaced with sitting still for a few minutes. Your new self-awareness and a greater sense of oneness may not fit the model of who you thought you were. You begin to change the way you feel about yourself.

I had the great pleasure of discussing this chapter with Amanda Freed, L.M.T., R.Y.T, C.M.T. Amanda is an amazing Yogini, massage therapist, and intuitive healer. She noted that participating in retreats or engaging in new practices of any kind can heighten emotional and physical sensitivity as you are spending more time learning about yourself and your 'self' on a higher and deeper level.

During the process of incorporating a consistent meditation practice, you also experience a shift. Shift is defined in the Merriam-Webster

Dictionary[16] as "(v) to put something aside and replace it by another or others; change or exchange." Amanda described the shift as a process of putting the old belief system of persona aside and bringing in a new you or a new expression of yourself. This deep connection to 'self' is different in every person.

This connection includes dropping judgments about 'self,' life experiences that no longer serve us, and all the mess that life piles up on us. The call to initiate a shift may differ. It could be sadness, a life event, or something or someone in your life. Something comes to life and calls on your inner self. You then create a relationship with that self. At that point, you can begin to live life from that place or spend more time in that place in a deeper consciousness. Your inner life begins to shift. You start to question. You research different levels of consciousness. As the shift takes hold, the outer level begins to shift as well. The beginning will seem like the biggest shift. And, of course, the most difficult. You are moving from nothing to something. We refer to this process as 'purification.' As you become more aware of what is happening, here are some things you may encounter:

- Loss

- Pain

- Abandonment

- Re-evaluation of toxic and/or negative relationships

The shifting process happens a lot in our lives. It can happen through therapy, new relationships, weight loss, etc. In the beginning of the process, there are gains and new insights. As you go along, the changes may be less profound, but they are still happening. For me, I felt less reactive and more peaceful. Unsolicited, my children also acknowledge how much happier and calmer I was. I did not notice the changes at first until I stopped

---

16 New Edition © 2016, January 1, 2016 by Merriam-Webster.

meditating for a week. I found myself feeling off and reactionary. I began to think more about my inner and outer selves.

What do we mean by "inner" and "outer" selves? Here are some examples:

- "Inner" self
- Ability to witness your own thought process
- Personal practices
- Belief systems
- "Outer" self
- How you spend your time
- Who you spend your time with
- What activities you are doing
- The food you eat
- What entertainment or reading material you enjoy

Purification is a by-product of shifting.

Purification means, according to the dictionary,[17] "To make pure: remove or free from contaminants."

When you purify yourself, you are freeing yourself from extraneous objectionable elements. All of the things that sit on your spirit and hold you back from being the person that you truly are. The process itself can be messy. It's like cleaning the garage – think of all the dirt and contaminates that get kicked up when you do it. But then what's left is cleaner, purer. Purification allows you to transform and shift from oneself to another. The process of purification is well worth it. Don't worry – it's worth the changes. It isn't easy.

---

17 Merriam-Webster Dictionary, New Edition © 2016, January 1, 2016 by Merriam-Webster.

And not everyone will experience a drastic change. Like everything in life, your experience is unique to you. My experience discovering my 'self' will not be the same as yours. We are two totally different people. You may not recognize any changes at all. Meditation is not a one size fits all process. It's a leap of faith. There is a natural and continued growth that never ends. The meditation is doing all of the work. You do the work of showing up, and meditation takes it from there. It can be hard. Try to be self-compassionate. Don't push yourself beyond the capacity of your own soul. Be gentle with your 'self' and your loved ones as you undergo this practice. It is important to be able to sit still with whatever is moving within you. At the same time, you need to be able to take a step back from the feeling or sensation if it is too much for you to handle.

One thing you will gain from the meditation process is "non-attachment." Non-attachment involves the ability to take a step back from whatever happens or whatever you are feeling. You acknowledge that the event or feeling is transient. You accept that it will soon change and transform. This quality of non-attachment is significant because it helps us not to get carried away with the drama of life, and to remain calm and peaceful in the chaos that surrounds us.

Try to remember: the non-attachment process is not the same as avoiding, repressing, or disregarding anything. DO NOT detach yourself from the people and activities you love and enjoy. Neither should you become passive or inactive. Non-attachment simply changes the quality of the relationship with life: it allows you to make conscious and peaceful choices. Not all the stuff that comes up is true, and not all the stuff that comes up requires attention. For me, I enjoyed my solitude more than ever. I felt like my time was better spent with positive people. I believe that "like brings like." I wanted more positive people to enter my life. Surrounding myself with drama, arguing, backstabbing, excessive alcohol, drugs, and people with agendas made for an environment full of things that made me sad and less tolerable. Your sensibilities will be different: do what is right for you.

I felt like I was nesting. I wanted to clean the energy around me. I gave things away that I had not used in a while. I set up space for a meditation area.

I would be remiss if I did not mention the loved ones, co-workers, and people with whom you surround yourself. And those who may or may not meditate. We must show kindness and compassion to them as well. We need to explain to them how our 'self' is transforming, so they understand what they are dealing with.

You might say, "I am growing, and I want you to be a part of this growth with me." It can be perplexing for them as well. Be patient with them as well as with yourself. Share your changes with your partner and the people in your life, and be active.

Here are some of the possible physical and emotional changes you may or may not experience while you go through this process:

Negative Emotional:

- Anger
- Sadness
- Anxiety
- Doubt
- Social isolation, a feeling of disconnect
- Disconnect from all the things you knew
- Irritability
- Oversensitivity
- Confusion
- Difficulty with energy and how to use it
- Positive Emotional:

- Connecting with others: like brings like
- Getting to your highest self
- Greater inner directedness
- Changes in attitude about life
- Self-actualization
- Learning forgiveness
- Deepened capacity to love
- Growing wisdom
- Discovering your purpose
- Deepened self-awareness
- Developing intuition and strengthening instincts
- Increased resilience against pain and adversity
- Greater inner-directedness
- A sense of "oneness"
- Increased self-esteem and self-compassion
- Improved relationships at home and work
- Elevated mood and happiness
- More control over your own thoughts
- Increased empathy
- Bliss – as you fall in love with yourself

PHYSICAL SYMPTOMS (see a doctor if they become chronic)

- Pain
- Sleeplessness
- Headaches

A meditation practice is a nourishing, healing process. However, if someone is facing difficulties and seeking help, meditation might not offer the support they are hoping for. It might be that they need to see a therapist to feel heard and understood.

Both meditation and therapy are associated with personal transformation. However, they work completely differently. There is no thinking during meditation. Therapy requires continued conversation and thinking. They both have their roles in the transformation process and may work in partnership. Some of the things you might experience through therapy are:

- Thinking about past and present issues

- Re-experiencing past and present issues

- Analyzation of past and present issues in order to move on from them

In contrast, during meditation when thoughts come up they are not analyzed. Rather, "alchemy[18]" makes these changes and purifies them. Meditation is a process that just happens. If you are willing and consistent, it will happen naturally.

When you are meditating, you aren't over-thinking patterns that exist. You are only focused on the *present*. Meditation is the cleansing of these thoughts. Therapy is the dissection and understanding of these repetitive patterns in order to move ahead and away from dysfunction to form a healthier lifestyle.

If you are having emotional issues that require addressing in therapy, check with your medical doctor for a referral.

CYNTHIA'S SEXY BRAIN FACTS

---

18 For these purposes, "alchemy" is defined as a process by which the spirit is purified.

- The smell of chocolate increases the theta brain waves which make you feel relaxed!

- Orgasms during sex trigger dopamine. Brain scans of people experiencing orgasms resemble those of someone who has ingested heroin.

- Music triggers dopamine as does eating and shopping.

- Sleeping pills don't actually put you to sleep. They put your brain into a similar state as a coma.

- Nicotine in tobacco smoke reaches the brain in seven seconds: it takes 6 minutes for alcohol to reach your brain.

- Despite what you might see in internet memes, we are not "left" or "right" brained – we are whole brained.

- Whales have bigger brains than humans.

- The brains of males are, on average, 10% bigger. (Remember – size doesn't always matter!)

- Multitasking slows down productivity and decreases memory, learning, and attention span.

- Yawning is the best way to send oxygen to the brain and wake it up.

- Lack of sleep hinders your ability to make new memories. (Remember this if you are studying for a test!)

- Most people dream 1-2 hours per night. However, after 10 minutes we forget 90% of our dream.

- We can't dream if we snore!

- The average brain generates 70,000 thoughts a day. In most people, 70% of those thoughts are negative.

- Laughing requires five parts of the brain working together at the same time.

CHAPTER EIGHT

ALL EARS: HOW TO DEEPLY LISTEN AND BE HEARD

"The truth you believe and cling to makes you unavailable to hear anything new."

~Pema Chodron

Do you ever wonder if anyone in your life is listening to anything that you are saying? So many times when I am trying to communicate with someone else I think – or, occasionally, say out loud – "Hello! I am talking to you!" It often feels like I am talking to someone's open palm, as in the rude, but common, gesture "Talk to the hand!" Even if someone wasn't completely tuning me out, I often felt like I was involved in a "half in/half out" conversation.

I remember often trying to have a conversation with my significant other. As I was talking, there was no eye-to-eye contact. He was on his computer or moving things around his desk. All the while, he would insist he was "listening" to the entire conversation, but I knew better. Sometimes I would be in the car driving and talking to him on the phone. He would only say a word or two, clearly not engaged in the conversation.

Does this sound familiar? It can happen at home, at work, or in any social situation. In the end, it feels like you are just talking to the air around you. I used to get so frustrated when I felt like no one was listening. I was being shut down even before I started. It was not until my mindfulness increasingly came into my life that I reset my communication and listening skills. This perspective was life changing. The calmness and clarity that comes from meditating strengthens us emotionally. We become more empathetic, and less reactive and affected by small everyday communication issues in our relationships.

The key to happiness includes harmonious relationships and open communication.

To me, mindful communication is getting the most out of your interactions with other people. Being mindful when you communicate requires you to connect with the experience of the moment, no matter what activity. When you say that you are listening, are you really fully present in the interaction with the person in front of you? Are you understanding what is being communicated to you?

Here are some mindful communication points to consider:

- As a mindful listener, respect that all interactions are equal. Your thoughts are just as important as mine.

- The people that we interact with are all fighting some sort of battles in their lives. They have big challenges both at home and at work, and they, too, are frustrated by daily petty annoyances.

- The emotions of those you interact with are as valid as yours. Sympathize with where they are coming from and show appreciation for what they feel.

- Through mindful communication, we can expand, grow, learn, and change. Even conflict provides us with the opportunity for self-discovery.

Be mindful of your voice. Observe your tone and volume. Voice tone sets the mood for any conversation. Your tone of voice communicates and creates a different emotion that people can hear. Do you raise your voice as a response to the feeling as if you are not being heard? Yelling seems to happen naturally for most people. Our adrenalin is released as a reaction to our frustration, anger, or stress. Instinctively, we have a tendency to allow our voices to become louder and more forceful. It's our way of creating dominance over the person you are speaking to. We raise our voice is an effort to talk over the other person. "I am going to talk over you so that I will FORCE YOU TO LISTEN TO WHAT I AM SAYING!" In reality, however, raising your voice only leads to high levels of negative feelings on both sides. Both people feel misunderstood and unacknowledged. When you feel your tone changing, slow down. Take a few long exhalations to calm your body. Relax your eyes, throat, and heart. This will naturally soften your tone.

It's important to explore our own communication patterns and how they are perceived by other people. For example, when I am feeling as if I am not being heard, am I also contributing to this lack of conversation? Why am I not connecting with this person right in front of me? How we relate to people will lead us on a path of self-discovery. Observing our communication patterns will increase our insights and awareness. Communications have a flow similar to traffic. They go back and forth in each person's direction. They are balanced. If they aren't going back and forth in balance, consider: why the traffic jam?

When I walk into my partner's office to have a conversation, one of three communication patterns will occur:

1. Open: This is a two-way conversation. It has the following characteristics: openness, open-mindedness; both parties paying attention, curiosity, empathy, shared compassion, a back and forth flow, and mutual interest.

2. Closed: He is not listening. There is defensiveness, and he is – or we are - opinionated. He has little or no interest in actual communication, in what I have to say. Barriers go up, and information is blocked. I am only thinking of my fears, reactions, projections, and my own mental storyline.

3. In-between: This is a hybrid pattern. There may be elements of open and closed conversation. It may fluctuate between one or the other.

Why is this important as a mind tool? Mindful communication will enable you to identify what I call "Red Light Triggers." Have you ever worked with someone or had a relationship with someone who immediately triggered a closed communication pattern inside of you? Someone who makes you just shut down as soon as they open their mouths and the first word comes out? Maybe you have relationships with a few people with whom you have had an instant rapport. You feel safe to communicate freely. Mindfulness will help you observe these communication patterns. Do you recognize when you are putting up barriers and thinking your own thoughts instead of listening to the person in front of you?

Mindful communication tools will also give you the power and control to avoid acting impulsively and making matters worse. You will be able to take a pause and hold steady during a conversation when you are disappointed, angry, or hurt. In the workplace, when a conversation between you and a coworker is not going as you hoped, you can avoid taking it personally and remain silent. This will prevent you from saying something you may later regret.

Closed communications occur when we have the belief "Me First!" When you think, "I will hold on to my ideas and opinions: our relationship is not that important." Closed communicators are only concerned with their own needs. They are selfish and have little empathy. They do not think twice about the impact their words have on other people. It is their way *or else*.

Closed communication results in increased stress and anxiety levels, isolation, frustration, and sadness. Basically, you feel undervalued by the person in front of you. That is not a warm, fuzzy feeling. Each of us reacts differently when being faced by closed communication. I used to turn inwards. When I felt like my husband was not listening to me, I gave up and shut down as well. I cut off communication from people with whom I did not feel a natural flow of energy.

Open communication, on the other hand, brings us connection and value. You get a sense of warmth, and there is more natural trust. It flows, and it goes! It's heartfelt, paying attention to the present conversation, sharing pain and joy, good and bad. You can agree and disagree while listening without thinking only of what you want to say back.

The in-between communication patterns are the warnings or reminders to slow down. Listen to what your gut is saying for a minute. What is going on inside of you that makes you want to go from an open to a closed conversation? I feel myself shutting down and not wanting to listen. I lose my connectedness. Is this trust based? Am I heading from "we first" to "me first?" When we find ourselves here, we should be aware that it is a signal for us to be mindful of our own sensitivities, anxieties, and patience levels. Your pause becomes your moment of choice. Which direction should you go? Should you hold on to the anger? Apologize? You have a choice whether to feel anger or disappointment or find a way to turn those feelings around in a positive way. Ask yourself these questions: Have I lost my perspective? Am I more concerned about promoting or protecting my own interests than listening to you?

Mindful listening is a skill that needs to be taken seriously. We live in a world filled with internal and external distractions. There is so much to distract us in our lifestyles, filled with multitasking and noise. These distractions hinder our abilities to understand and build a connection with one another.

Watch other families at restaurants. Are they giving each other eye contact? Are they actively listening to each other? Or are they staring at their cell phones? It's rare that we hear an entire conversation. Often, it is just bits and pieces. There are so many external interferences that grab our attention. Our need for dopamine and novelty is competing with your conversation. Millions of dollars are lost to companies every year due to unnecessary mistakes and missed opportunities that directly result from poor listening. Researchers have found that approximately 40% of our waking hours are spent listening to people. Yet the average person can only recall 25% of what they heard.[19]

- Listening is in itself a process and a skill. You are not listening if:

- You are thinking about listening.

- You are preparing your response in your mind while the other person is still talking.

- You are interrupting the speaker.

- You tune the person out because you disagree with his or her beliefs.

- You are daydreaming.

- You are not maintaining eye contact with the speaker.

Listening is a skill that takes time and dedication. It requires a balance between focus of attention and open-mindedness and tolerance of different views. Think about the political climate today. Most people are just not listening to one another. Most people are instantly shut down when they hear you voted for the 'other' candidate. Therefore, your opinions and statements are also not worthwhile, whether or not they are related to your political differences. After just a few seconds of time, we have judged whether or not to listen. This creates a resistance to the message and a disconnect to the speaker.

- Mindful listening involves the following:

- Finding a connection with the experience of the present moment.

- Feeling an emotional connection with the speaker.

- Finding motivation in the words that are being said.

- Letting go of bias, distractions, and negative self-talk.

---

19 "The Five Keys to Mindful Communication: Using Deep Listening and Mindful Speech to Strengthen Relationships, Heal Conflicts, and Accomplish Your Goals." Paperback, April 10, 2012, by Susan Gillis Chapman.

- Training yourself to be present and avoiding a wandering mind.

Pay attention to yourself when you speak and when you listen. Are you really listening? If you are, if you are really letting the speaker be the anchor for your attention, you will find your conversations to be much more rewarding. Don't undercut the communication before it has a chance to begin. Rather, look for the synergy you share with the people you are talking to.

CHAPTER NINE

DON'T SHOULD ON YOURSELF

"In any kind of relationship we can make the assumption that others know what we think, and we don't have to say what we want. They are going to do what we want because they know us so well. If they don't do what we want, what we assume they should do, we feel hurt and think, 'How could you do that? You should know.' Again, we make the assumption that the other person knows what we want. A whole drama is created because we make this assumption and then put more assumptions on top of it."

~Miguel Ruiz, "The Four Agreements: A Practical Guide to Freedom."

Throughout my life, even when things were at the worst, so many friends and family members of mine would ask how I managed to stay so positive. "How are you not negative or resentful?" they'd ask. "How did you prevent yourself from just giving up?"

The first response I had was that giving up and throwing in the towel was simply not an option for me. And then I would explain further, condensing what I learned from reading many books and from my therapy practice. I start with knowing what side of the line I'm on, or what side of the door I enter into when a situation occurs.

Before I go further with this concept, note that there isn't a right or wrong way of dealing with situations that occur in your life. In fact, it is completely normal for people to live their life in a "should" lifestyle. In this mindset, the world is the way you think it should be. Your kids should obey. Your employees and coworkers should be productive. You should have known better. The majority of people on this planet really believe that there is a way that people should or should not be.

Here's the problem, with that: life and its events do not always unfold the way they should. When that happens, most people react by becoming anxious, fearful, or controlling. We have a tendency to try to force the world to fit into our "should" beliefs. When you do that – how does it work out for you? Most people blame –blame themselves, other people, or just the circumstances themselves. The last thing we consider doing is taking responsibility, which is not the same as self-blame. Blame is negative – it is assigning *fault*. Taking responsibility means having an understanding that the choices you've made and the situations you've put yourself in have led to your current position. This can be positive, even if your current position is negative since you have now learned, through trial and error, what those choices will lead to.

Believe it or not, it goes right back to the almond – yup, the amygdala. It stands guard, analyzing each perception and every situation. It asks, "Could this bring me harm, danger, or pleasure?" It is the protector and is in charge of your survival. If we sense a threat to our ego, it's a natural reaction to get defensive.

So, when a situation occurs in our lives, we more often than not choose one of two lenses with which to view the situation:

1. The situation is caused by an external force outside of me. *External* realities are responsible.

2. You take responsibility for the circumstances you face, for whatever is occurring in your life, and you let go of the idea that someone or something is to be blamed.

For example, when I discovered I was about to lose my house, I had two ways to look at the situation at hand.

1.

Why is this happening to me?
This is all of my husband's fault.
Who is going to fix this?
Someone is to blame, and it isn't me!

The cause and control of this problem is outside of myself.

2.

What am I learning from this?
How am I helping to create this situation?
How am I keeping this going in my life?
This is a lesson or, in the end, a blessing.
What are the wins here?

Understandably, the majority of us choose the blaming, defensive route. We feel the need to keep our egos intact. For this, blame it all on the "almond." We allow the grip of conscious fear and anxiety to cause us to be reactive. The "shoulds" take over. We believe our life's experiences are outside of ourselves and our control. Blame becomes a strong motivator. It's your fault, my fault, and the world's fault.

But maybe there is a way to take a peek at this from another angle. Another 'shift' of sorts. Instead of a closed minded, defensive mindset, consider a mindset of openness and curiosity. Whatever the circumstance that is occurring in your life, take responsibility for it and release the need to blame someone or something. Open yourself to learning what life is trying to teach you. Let go of the control of the situation and the people that you were not really meant to control in the first place. Get rid of the "shoulds." They lead only to disempowerment, reactivity and, ultimately, unhappiness.

If you find yourself thinking the following thoughts, just stop:

The world should be a certain way.

I need to be right.

To avoid conflict, I will do more than 100%.

This is out of my control.

This is not fair.

Instead, replace those unhelpful thoughts with the following ones:

It's really an opportunity to learn what the world is teaching me.

Both good and bad experiences allow me to grow and learn more about myself.

No matter what is happening in my life, I can still find gratitude.

We create our own experiences in life. No situation or person is doing it to us.

I am solely responsible for my emotional, physical, mental, and spiritual well-being.

Self-awareness and knowing what side of the line or door you choose to enter is vital to your mindset. Yes, I could have just blamed all of my challenges on the people around me. I could have played the victim role. I could have blamed the economy, or my luck, or the fact that I lived in California. I could have felt angry and resentful. Instead, I knew all of the blame would lead to disempowerment. Blame gives someone or something else control over your circumstances and emotions. I wanted to grow and understand more about myself and what role I played in the process. I gave total financial control to a man that I trusted to take care of my children and me. That was something that I did. Recognizing that, I picked the side of the line that helped me to understand how everything in life is a learning opportunity and has value.

Don't let "shoulds" run your life.

How often in any given day do you use the word "should?" One day I tallied the number of times I said it. I was taken aback by the number, 23 times! The next day, I tallied the number of times I heard other people saying it.

What is so awful about using that word? Dr. Albert Ellis coined the terms "shoulding" and "musterbating." Just saying those words aloud should (ha ha) give you a mindful tickle. "Musterbating" is used to describe the phenomenon where people live by a set of absolute and unrealistic demands that they place on themselves, others and the world – the way things "must" be. For most of us, these rules come out in a series of "should" statements – that's "shoulding." We repeat these "should" statements over and over again, and they leave us feeling bad about ourselves when the world doesn't conform to our expectations. When you find yourself "shoulding," remind yourself that while it may be nice to reach your goals and be treated the way you want, we are all human and live in an imperfect world. Therefore, the pressure to be anything or to expect consistency all the time is more likely to cause harm than good. The world "must" not or "should" not be anything – it simply is.

"Should" is an instrument of regret. It's not an easy word to remove from your vocabulary. We seem to have picked that word up early in life, and immediately place the "should" card front and center when things don't go according to plan. This results in self-blame. There is clearly something wrong with us. These are the worst kind of "shoulds" that we impose on ourselves. "Shoulds" lead to increased frustration and lowers our motivation and productivity. "Shoulds" also create unrealistic and irrational expectations of ourselves and others. We tend to judge other people's actions and get annoyed when they don't "act right." The people around us, we tell ourselves, should know and obey the rules as we have defined them. This demandingness leads to anger, hurt, and self-pity.

"Shoulds" are limiting. When you feel yourself saying the word, take note and immediately pause. Remind yourself that this is a great opportunity to examine what is happening in the moment. Greater insights can happen when we look closely enough. Embrace your self-discovery, even though it can be difficult. Start by catching yourself when you say should have/could have/would have/what if/if I had/why did I say/why didn't he do and, of course, the completely illogical "If I had, then never would have" mindset.

Tips on breaking the "should" habit:

- Write a list of the things you think you should be doing today and all this week. Feel the freedom of writing any of the "shoulds" that you can think of and that surface for you. Keep a log of the "should" that you find yourself saying during the day. "I need to lose ten pounds." "I should write a chapter this week." "I should get ready faster." "I should call my friend." "I should go visit my father, even though I don't want to." "I should eat healthier foods."

- Go through your list. I read mine aloud to make sure I didn't skip anything and to make sure I was paying attention. After you read each "should," ask yourself, "Why should I?" This will help you to see where these obligations are coming from. Then you can actively decide in the grand scheme of things whether these "shoulds" are really important, or if they just *feel* important.

- Think about what is behind the "should." "I should go to the party." Do you really want to go? Do you feel like you should because someone else's feeling would be hurt? Because it is a good networking opportunity? Think about your reasoning. Are you reluctant to make a change in your life that involves you taking control of change and the outcome? Are you really feeling guilty that you are not living up to other's expectations of you? "Shoulds" are tricky little buggers, full of subtle nuance – they hold us back while also alerting us. They let us know that we are not doing we want, even when we are unwilling to change it.

- Change the way you word things – both out loud and in your thoughts. Review the list. This time, replace the "shoulds" with phrases like, "If I really wanted to, I could..." and "I prefer" and "I would like it if."

- As yourself: what really matters to me right now?

- Are these expectations that I place upon myself going to bring about the changes I want to see in the world? Can I find a better way than this?

- Trust yourself!

As you process the use of "shoulds" and where you fall in terms of taking responsibility for your personal growth, consider Miguel Ruiz's book *The Four Agreements*. These are powerful mind tools. Ruiz wrote these agreements with the belief that as we enter this world, we are born loving, genuine, and playful. However, as children, we are taught beliefs, both positive and negative, from our parents and other authority figures in our lives. We do and say the 'right' things that we are taught because it helps us to fit in and have our needs met. We want to please our parents and teachers. As kids, we have no choice but to agree to what the adults are telling us to believe. If you say that I am pretty, then I am. If you say that I am worthless, then I must be that, too.

So, I am offering you a chance to replace or break away from your previous agreements and look inside yourself for direction. You have the freedom to adopt new agreements that will allow you to express yourself more freely. It will allow you to connect to who you are and get rid of the self-doubt that fuels your fears.

Agreement #1. Be impeccable with your word. How do you use words against yourself? How do you judge yourself? Can you perform, desire, or feel emotions without judging yourself? If we act on what we tell ourselves is real, what negative self-talk are you using? Here comes that mind-chatter again. Do you say negative things about yourself and others? Is it worth placing your energy in such a negative space? It is better to be honest with ourselves and others and have a positive influence and energy that surrounds you. Like brings like. If you want more positive energy around you, start with giving off positive energy. Have you ever noticed that when you are excited to share some positive news with your co-workers that the energy in the room shifts and starts to feel better? Now think about a friend or co-worker who is miserable and constantly complains. Can you feel the difference? Before you know it, other people start to chime in, and the negative energy increases, becoming more and more difficult to shake off. The negative thoughts will stay longer in your brain than the positive ones. That's why we tend to wallow in a bad mood much longer than we can sustain a good mood when we are over-the-moon happy.

Agreement #2. Don't take things personally. This is a tough one, but it can be achieved. Someone's opinion has nothing to do with you. It's based on their own distorted beliefs and personal agreements. In reality, it is independent of you. Don't own someone's painful or hurtful treatment of others. Not taking things personally is really accepting the unique qualities of other people. All of us have our own subjective realities and views. Let's agree that your view of me may not accurately describe me as I see myself. In the end, you do not walk in my shoes. So, I am going to be myself in a way that feels right to me. Your description of me has nothing to do with me. I will not take it personally. If the person sitting next to you tells you they do not like your shirt, instead of being insulted think, "Do I like my shirt?" "Do I feel happy in that shirt?" In the end, your own personal opinion is all you need. It does not matter if someone likes you or what you are doing at all It's more important that you like yourself. When you take things personally, it really means that you are in an agreement with the other person about what they are saying to you.

Agreement #3. Don't make assumptions. How I wish that I could put this one over a loudspeaker! DO NOT ASSUME WHAT THOSE AROUND YOU ARE THINKING, FEELING, OR DOING!!! Do NOT second guess. Are you a mind reader? No, of course not. Assumption leads to misunderstandings, undesired consequences, and generally stepping into bad stuff. I recently encountered a friend who made assumptions about my intentions. He didn't think I was spending enough time with him and jumped to conclusions about why. He didn't ask me questions or call me to share his concerns. Instead, he sent a rude text. Had he asked me what was going on, we would still be friends. Instead, he allowed his imagination to take over and create a story. This fulfilled his 'need to know' and replaced his need to communicate. Don't make the assumption that I know what is on your mind. If you want to know what I want or what I'm thinking, ASK ME. Don't be afraid of hurting someone's feelings because you assume that you should know what they need. Just ask! How many gifts do you have stored away from people who made assumptions about what you like? Calculate how many times you made assumptions that were just plain wrong. Asking questions is connecting and growing. Communicate and keep on asking until you are clear about any situation. Let's be clear and let your voice be heard. I will know what you want, and you will know what I want.

Agreement #4. Always do your best. Achieve your goals by working smarter, not harder. Avoid your internal judgment. Know that what is "the best" will be different from moment to moment. Whatever you do, don't let this agreement to "do your best" give you license to beat yourself up or push yourself too hard. It's really there to remind you that you have the choice to be the best you can be in the present. Incorporate your knowledge from your previous experiences in order to change and grow. Rid yourself of your negative self-talk about your past failures and the shoulda coulda woulda's. Be the best that you can presently be. No more and no less. If you try too hard, then you overuse your energy. You become depleted, and you won't have energy stores when you need them. Doing your best makes you happy. It's the joy of the action of what you are doing, not the reward at the end. It is living fully and taking the risk to follow your dreams. Learn from your challenges and mistakes, accept yourself, and increase your self-awareness. We are only limited by the limits we place on ourselves by our beliefs.

***

"Shoulds," assumptions, negative talk, and gossip all lead to toxicity and undermine our lives. They create stress, add worry, and contribute to clouding our thinking. The negativity takes over our lives. Before we know it, we have self-sabotaged and gotten into our own way. This results in a restricted path in which we are unable to build successful relationships. Failures and mishaps are nothing more than an opportunity. We all make mistakes. Remember, though that *we are not the mistakes we make.* We cannot take defeats personally. We cannot internalize our mistakes and our past choices.

Don't allow mistakes to become an opportunity to feed into your usual negative self-talk or to bolster a negative mindset. The pile of negativity will end up becoming an insurmountable mountain. I am too afraid of heights to climb that lofty a peak. In the end, I took the challenges and failures in my life and saw them as learning experiences. I had many of these kinds of learning experiences! It was my commitment to growth. Yup, I fell flat on my face. More than once. But I could not stay on the floor forever. I had to get up and move. When everything in your life is gone, everything changes. The physical and mental boundaries that previously surrounded me were gone. It took mindfulness to help me stand back and examine my self-judgments and observe on which side of the line I stood.

Take the time to examine the agreements and beliefs that you have about yourself. Do they empower you? Do they limit you? How you see your world will play into your mental, physical, and emotional energy of your day. It will raise you up or deplete you completely. Your mindset when you jump (or roll) out of bed each day will stay with you until you retire to bed that same night. Start your day with thoughts of gratitude.

CHAPTER TEN

UNDERSTANDING THE BIG 3

"What we think, we become." – *Buddha*

So there I was. I was in my 50's, an empty nester on my second divorce, without any clue what the future held for me. Leaving Carlos was hard, but I had no choice. I had to figure out what to do next.

My first task at hand was finding a place to live. Finding a house was no easy feat. I had just a few weeks before homelessness to find a house on the water that allowed pets and had lots of light and amazing views. I wrote all of the criteria I had for the house on a piece of paper – what I liked and wanted, and what I disliked and did not want. I knew that I needed to be tucked in somewhere cozy like a cocoon. I needed to be free from the distractions of a busy life. I didn't want to be too close to friends, family, social, entertainment, shopping, or the beach. I didn't want the temptation of distraction. I was committed to myself. I would take a year off and truly connect with my soul, spirit, mind, and heart.

Eventually, the house I found actually found me. It was my first leap of faith. I saw the house once after touring many houses. It was peaceful and met all the criteria on my list. I remember thinking, "Well, if it is meant to be it will be." It was a secluded house on a sod farm outside of Annapolis, Maryland.

Starting out in this house was not easy. My children had just been booted out of a house they had been promised they could stay in. I was forced to leave a place I considered my home. The owner of the sod farm had left a lot of his possessions, and I not only had to move my stuff in but pack up his stuff and get it out of the way. On moving day, after all of my stuff was carried in, I sat in a chair and cried. What had I done? I was too far from civilization. I was off the beaten path. My closest friend was an hour away. It was dark and spooky at night. What if it snowed? Where did all of my positive thoughts go? That almond and seahorse were beating me up! The self-talk and negative recordings in my head were blasting at full volume. That darned negative bias in my brain. I counted the days until my lease would expire. I would not allow myself to connect with the house.

I couldn't understand why all my friends thought it was the perfect house for me. I wondered how I allowed myself to move there. It made me angry. I had house blessings, I burned sage and purified the house as best I could. I lit vanilla candles and had fresh flowers on hand. I played my favorite music. At the same time, I resisted the impulse to internalize my positive feeling for this house and what it represented.

Instead of being mindful and feeling grateful, I felt stuck and fearful. I didn't see that I needed to become familiar with fear and stop running from it. Fear was at the core of all my past challenges. I knew this, yet I was allowing fear to come right back in, wipe its feet on the welcome mat, and take over my life. Talk about repeating destructive patterns! Look where those patterns got me in the past. I hid. I became small in myself and my posture. I was worn out and too overwhelmed to be in my present. I did not understand that my failure to protect myself mentally and physically was hindering my mindfulness and my power.

When we feel like the rug is being taken out from beneath us, we are thrown from the nest and have no clue what will happen next – will we fly, or will we fall to the ground? It's an opening to be able to see things more clearly. However, we tend to retreat to old habits and thinking, and we get anxious and start to weave our old stories into strong rope. This makes our emotions even bigger. They become inflamed and hot. We can't let go.

Fear is a universal experience. It's something we are all familiar with. We often feel fear when we are faced with unknown situations. We fear death and being alone, becoming unable to take care of ourselves. We see only our rejections and our financial burdens. In this state of mind, I sat in a chair, immobilized. Being alone and looking at my present situation made things appear magnified. I wondered how I would be able to support myself. I wondered if I would find love, if I would be happy and at peace with myself again. A whole board of failures was a poster on the wall, right in front of me. And I was the one who placed it there.

When our lives are not going in the direction we thought they should be, fear is always in the front of the line, waiting to jump in and rattle us.

Courageous people know fear. Courage is not the absence of fear. Rather, courage is the ability to look fear in the face and proceed on despite the fear. It allows you to confront your old ways of hearing, seeing, thinking, and acting. We can have an intimate relationship with fear. It can guide us to move closer to our truth.

I knew my truth and my triggers. I just had to face them.

*　*　*

Everyone has dealt with their lives falling apart on some level. Life is without guarantees and constantly changing. My life was not as I expected it to be. It unraveled differently than I thought it would. But, where there is a test, there is a healing opportunity. You can choose panic or the present; uncertainty or dependency. These are all choices. When we are feeling vulnerable and in a sensitive place, we can either shut down and be resentful and angry, or we can open our hearts, stay in the present, and become a peaceful warrior.

We heal more often than we think. How many times in your life have you witnessed things falling apart and then getting back together? Then something else falls apart and gets back together again. Transitions occur in our jobs, relationship, finances, plans, and opportunities. This allows more space for grief, joy, love, happiness, anger, relief, and freedom.

I truly thought I was going to be in a happy, long-term, stable relationship. I opened myself up and trusted and had faith in someone who made me feel safe. At the same time, repeated patterns of dependency and enabling showed themselves. Instead of what I expected, I entered a new situation of uncertainty. I had no clue how my life story would end. But this disappointment has lead me to a huge adventure.

Hiding under the covers and feeling hopeless will not give you the comfort and safety you think it will. The ground is still moving around us. It feeds into abdicating our responsibilities and delegating our authority to something outside ourselves. The sad reality is that there is no one you can really count on, and there is no security in life. You should expect the unexpected. Nothing stays the same. Learn to rely on yourself – be your own friend.

The second day in the house, I thought about how far I had come over the last six months. I began to ask myself basic questions. Am I ok? Am I safe? Do I have a roof over my head for myself and my kids? Do I have resources to call upon? Have I been in worse situations? Am I being a peaceful warrior? Where are the wins? What are my inner strengths? Am I being a role model for my kids? Is this how I want my life to continue? The list of questions continued for hours. It was just two weeks before Christmas. Where was my holiday spirit? A new year was coming. New beginnings were sprouting everywhere. I opened my heart and mind. I took the opportunity to use my mind tools to get moving.

In troubled times we undervalue our successes and exaggerate our failures and disappointments. This negative attitude, waiting for the other shoe to drop mentality, feeds into our new situations and opportunity. When something good happens, instead of owning it, we often pass it off to an external source and simple luck. If we stay in the present, however, we can have early detection of anxiety. We can communicate those anxieties and shrug them off more easily.

It's not uncommon to allow life's setbacks to allow us to feel a lot of fear. This fear just reinforces our sense of powerlessness and exhaustion. It locks us into a state of negativity. A sense of powerlessness is like shutting down our PFC and our executive functioning. Our lack of clarity clouds our abilities to meet the demand of complicated and stressful situations. The internal power we have has significant effects on our actions and thoughts. Our mind tools help us to increase our inner power by having unlimited access to our inner resources, skills, abilities, and our true selves, as bold as they are! We just need the confidence to act and feel our inner power in an authentic way. You can fake an orgasm, but not power!

Twice daily meditation allowed me to have a clarity to my feelings, thoughts, and emotions. It was time to look at my fears and see why I felt threatened inside of myself. Fear and anxiety was a signal to me that I was entering unknown territory alone. Pulling the covers over my head and staying immobile was *not* the answer, as tempting as it was. I had to step into my journey. I could not deny it or lay victim to it. There would be no easy road to sanity.

I found my warm, nurturing, secure space within meditation. Each day I welcomed my fears and anxiety while meditating. I became more aware of my life. The thoughts and emotions came, I acknowledged them, and I let them leave. Then, I would return to repeating my mantra. Through this year, I was slowly able to live a life of mindfulness. I was more relaxed. I found a lessening of negative self-talk, and increased my ability to find joy in the present moment. I was committed to a life of learning, growing, compassion, and connection. I wanted to consistently be on the joyful side of the line, learning and accepting. Life is not a bowl of cherries. I could dodge fear, hide from it, deny it, or find someone else to fix it. But what I needed to do was lean in and embrace my fears, along with the loss and embarrassment that went along with it.

Seeing what was happening to me made me a believer in the process. I increased my practice gradually to an hour a day. I love night time guided meditations, but I have to admit I fall asleep after only ten minutes. However, I have noticed that my sleep is much better and much less interrupted.

REFRAINING

Refraining is the method we use to get to know the nature of our restlessness and fear. If we immediately entertain or distract ourselves by thinking or talking or doing, if there is not a pause, we cannot relax. Refraining is the way we make friends with ourselves at the most profound level.

When we feel lonely, we feel hopeless. We don't want to sit and feel what we feel. Meditation is a way to train you to stay in the right spot. It is not a place to judge whatever arises in our minds. We allow the thoughts to come and go gently as if touching a bubble with a feather. We constantly look for resolutions with our feelings.

When we feel that we have a lot to lose, that feeling is rooted in fear. We fear loneliness and change, and anything else that can't be easily resolved. Do you freak out or settle into the belief that you have to give up when you are afraid? We have to let go of the belief that escaping loneliness is going to bring any lasting happiness or joy or sense of well-being, let alone courage or strength.

When we are lonely, we look for something or someone to save us. We come up with companions and activities to save us from despair. We keep ourselves busy, so we don't feel the pain. It's hard to settle down and have respect and compassion for ourselves. Relaxing with loneliness is a worthy occupation. You need to sit still long enough to realize how things really are. There is no certainty about much of anything – and that's ok.

Loneliness is not a punishment if you wake up and look at it as an opportunity. Instead of being upset with yourself or giving into sadness, try relaxing and touch the unlimited space in your heart.

OBSTACLES

Obstacles occur in relationships and in many other situations. When we confront them, we feel angry and confused and attacked in many ways.

Inner obstacles attack us with confusion. We don't like what is happening now, we want it to pass, and we try to let it go as soon as we can. But nothing ever goes away until it has taught us what we need to know. No matter where you go or hide, it just waits for you to arrive on the other side.

YOU are the only one that can change your habitual "stuckness." You have to stand up and keep walking. The waves will come, they will keep on coming, but they will feel smaller and smaller. If you lie there drowning, you will keep on drowning. It's how we keep ourselves miserable and stuck with an unhappy, limited view on reality.

It's tempting to stay in your small cocoon rather than experiencing the unknown thrill of stepping out into a big space. It's safe and predictable in our cocoons. It's convenient. We know where everything is. The furniture and the clothes we like are exactly where we put them. We like zones of safety. Our minds seek zones of safety. We scramble to go from one safety zone to another. But these zones continually fall apart.

"Samsara" is a Sanskrit word that literally translates to "wandering" or "world." But it also refers to a state in which the walls fall down, our cocoons completely disappear, and we are open to whatever is about to happen. We no longer draw into ourselves. We are thrown from the nest, leaping, stepping into something that is uncertain and unknown.

FEARS

We build so much of our lives around fears. Fears are normal and built in. They are part of our predisposition to avoid harm. Our fears, if we let them, permeate everything. Over time, just like self-talk, we develop fear patterns. When fear has more authority over our actions than we do, we are possessed by it. It can cause us to behave outside the boundaries of kindness and love. Fears are powerful because they are unreasonable and unnecessary. They gain a foothold in our unconscious and morph into irrational beliefs.

Since fear lives mostly in the future, leave it there. Stay in the present. Fears are in our mind. You have power and control over your fears. Never give up.

Do you consider your fears to be reasonable or unreasonable? Take this thought apart: what is the bottom line of your fear. Is your fear really greater than your faith in yourself and your abilities to handle it?

Learn to endure. Give up the need to know *why* things are happening. Everything is just an experience. Does this experience make you more aware? More grateful? Kinder? More empathetic? More compassionate?

Act on your own guidance without reminding yourself that you are afraid. Don't wait for or require proof that you will be safe. Every choice we make is a leap. Stop letting fear be the one constant voice you listen to with unremitting faith. Look at me – my house caught fire, I lost another to foreclosure, and my husband left me for another woman – one that he never even ended up with. I wear all these experiences as badges of courage. They give me the strength and determination to fight the next battle. I landed on my feet then, and I will do it again.

Fear will knock at your door when you are alone and at night. You are the only one that can open the door and entertain it. Fears grow from minute to minute and expand in our mindset. If we give energy to the reaction, we end up self-sabotaging ourselves.

Take a breath. Leave things small, and they will stay small. They won't be fed by the fire of negative self-talk and expend. It's transformative to simply pause instead of filling that space. By pausing, we begin to connect with our restlessness. We cease to cause harm to ourselves and – most importantly – we get to know and respect ourselves. With practice, it doesn't matter if something unexpected or uncertain pops up. We don't over react. Instead, we have more time and clarity to make a reasoned response.

We can't just sit and hope that the winds of change will pass us by. If we do this, we will only wait until our fears consume us, and we will deny our intuitive warning signals. Wisdom rises to meet the challenges of life. Woe is the result of thinking others will take care of your problems or that they will magically disappear. Your problems have your name on them. They are for you to resolve through wise action and the grace and light of your life.

PRESENCE

Social Psychologist Amy Cuddy describes presence as believing in yourself, and in your real, honest feelings, and your values and abilities. It's a powerful internal connection with yourself. Our negative bias seems to put a glitch in accurately assessing the positive in ourselves. It's ironic how easily we can feel fear and buy into it as we let it take over our minds and actions. However, our sense of powerfulness is not as easily taken in. If we can't love and trust ourselves, how can we expect other people to love and trust us?

Over this past year, I have learned that slowly, and only in small increments, you can embrace your power. Staying in your present and using your power is a mind tool that will help you when you are facing daily life challenges. Treat challenges as moments. "This, too, shall pass." Presence stems from believing our own stories. We need to focus less on impressing each other, and more on impressing ourselves by holding our focus. I feel my presence when there is a certain psychological alignment inside me.

Presence gives you the power to help others find their own presence during a challenging time. Staying in your present *is* mindfulness. If you are thinking about other things like a to-do list or trying to organize things, you are not being mindful. You are distracted and have lost your focus on being in the here and now.

Before you go into a stressful situation at work or home, first visualize your experience. What you see and feel will come true. If you see fear and dread, that's what energy you will bring in and manifest. If you bring confidence and knowledge instead, that will be the energy of the situation. You can't fake that energy – you really have to feel it. Your non-verbal clues will give you away.

You have to be able to comfortably express our true feelings, thoughts, strengths, values, and potential. This is not a permanent mode of being: it is transcendent. It will come and go.

Personally feel powerful. Attend to your sincere belief of self.

In your present, you are being yourself. It's an honest, powerful connection that we create internally within ourselves.

A lack of power makes us feel self-absorbed, with a lack of mental clarity. We experience anxiety, which in turn makes us unable to read a situation accurately. Power*ful*ness, on the other hand, protects us against negative emotions and stress, while building a connectivity with others. It liberates our thinking and strengthens our executive function while increasing our creativity and productivity. It also makes us feel shielded from external sources of pressure and criticism.

When we tilt towards the negative self-talk, we don't believe our stories, and therefore we are not being our authentic self. It lowers our confidence and is self-deceiving.

Our attitude and beliefs will enable or block our ability to see the best solution. You must believe in your signature strengths. It is so easy to get sucked into social dysfunction at the water cooler, but it is at these times that you can best motivate yourself to pull out your affirmations. You ground yourself in your own truth about your own stories. You become less dependent upon the approval of the other people you surround yourself with. Their disapproval will have a lessening effect.

Get to know yourself. Use more mind tool exercises. Write a list of affirmations that are the closest to your core strengths and your core identity. Keep them with you, tucked in a pocket, your wallet, or your purse, or in a document on your smartphone. Recite them often.

A heightened emotional state can increase cortisol. Increased cortisol creates anxiety spikes and stress and impairs social judgment. Why wouldn't you want to avoid this when you can?

If you carry your personal affirmations with you and say them ahead of time, you will have a sense of your personal values. This will decrease your cortisol levels. Affirming your core values also lowers your epinephrine levels, which are related to the "fight or flight" response. You don't want to fight or flight. You want a reasoned response.

Self-affirmations work best when the stakes are high.

Before entering a stressful situation where you may be challenged, you can greatly reduce your anxiety by reflecting on the parts of your authentic self that you value the most. When we feel safe with ourselves, we become significantly less defensive and more open to feedback. It makes us more efficient problem solvers.

Knowing who you are elevates your sense of meaning.

Spend time with yourself. Assemble your deepest self by reflecting and writing who you think you are. Build and believe in your story.

Own it.

Affirm it.

Believe it.

Take control of how you tell your story.

Presence exercises:

- List three words that best describe you as a person.

- List three signature strengths.

- Describe three separate situations and how you used your strengths.

- Write a brief paragraph about a time when you were acting that made you feel like your natural and right self. Think: how can you repeat this experience?

- Name five qualities or attributes about yourself that contributes to your happiest and best outcomes in your life. Think about how you can use those qualities or attributes more often.

SELF-COMPASSION

Self-compassion involves accepting yourself and all of your imperfections. That includes all of yourself, and your non-judgmental, open space. You must show compassion and love towards yourself. This is not the same thing as feeling sorry for yourself or self-pity. It is the recognition and discovery that in some big or small ways you are constantly hurting, stressing, burdening, or destroying yourself unnecessarily.

It's a matter of shifting your mindset. You have to take care of yourself first. It takes a while to get the hang of this, especially if you are a giving person. A giving person's life mission is to put other people's lives first. But, in the end, you have to love yourself first before you can even attempt to give yourself freely and love another person.

Do you question whether or not you are loveable? Do you seek out partners who validate you? No one is responsible for completing you or filling up your love tank. Just you. You are the best advocate for yourself. When you are on a plane and they review the safety instructions, who do they say should put on the oxygen mask first? You. You should put on your own oxygen mask before helping someone else because without that life force you can't help anyone else.

It has taken me most of my life to finally get this concept and let it sink in. I am responsible for me, and in the end, I am the only person I can depend upon. I enter the world alone and leave it the same way. Don't think of this as a scary or lonely thought – rather, it is self-affirming. You don't need anyone else but yourself.

Heal, and learn to love yourself. Self-kindness will replace self-judgment. Don't beat yourself up. There is enough negativity around. See that negative thinking is defeating, and therefore not motivating. It's a matter of shifting your thinking, going from being reactive to being responsive, from being greedy to being grateful.

Everyone has a bad day, week, or year. You have the power to control how much you allow this to drive you crazy. You have the power to reduce all of these reactions and outside resources that upset you. Everyone is in the same boat. It might not feel that way, but everyone has transitions, changes, and tough times. Picture a friend who is going through a hard time. Send them compassion and kindness. And, with the same level of compassion and kindness, you should give those feelings to yourself. Let them soak in like a sponge. Self-compassion leads to you feeling whole, validated, and accepting of yourself.

Self-compassionate people take responsibility for their actions, whether good or bad. Do you ever consider yourself special? You are one of a kind. There is not another person on the planet that looks like you or is wired the way you are on the inside. Honor who you are and your specialness.

Replace self-criticism with positive self-statements. Soften your harsh inner voices. Catch yourself. Take a pause and be aware when you refer to yourself in a negative way. Reach up, note the thought, and let it go. Then, when you've done that, reward yourself. When I start to tell myself, "I can't...." an alarm bell goes off in my head. Try a self-compassion meditation like the one that follows. It can really work!

LOVING KINDNESS SELF-COMPASSION MEDITATION

This practice should take 20-30 minutes. Find a comfortable position, either sitting or lying down. Let your eyes close, fully or partially. Gently follow the instructions.

- Take 3 or 4 deep breaths through your nose to settle into yourself.

- Let your breath return to its natural rhythm. Let your breath move through your body. Scan your body, relaxing as you go. Feel the gentle movement of your breath once again.

- After a few minutes, start to notice any physical sensations of stress that you may be holding in your body, perhaps in your neck, back, jaw, belly, or shoulders. Let go of whatever tension that you can.

- Loosen your shoulders. Soften your hands, and relax your belly. After you feel settled and relaxed, bring you attention to your heart center. If you feel comfortable doing so, place your hand gently on your heart.

- Visualize a smile in your mind. Begin to notice the kindness and joy and the ease at bringing this smile inside yourself.

- Now bring a smile to your face. A small smile, without tightening the muscles in your face. Do you feel the corners of your mouth smiling?

- Feel the openness and the vibrancy of your smile moving through your body.

- Focus again on your heart center. Open up your basic kindness. Bring to mind a time when you have been kind and generous. See yourself through the eyes of someone who loves and cares for you. What does that person love about you? Imagine this person or pet sending their love. They are also sending you good thoughts and their wishes for your well-being, happiness, and safety. Feel the warm wishes coming to you.

- Now imagine that you are sitting inside of a circle and you are surrounded by all of the people who love you and have loved you. Visualize your friends and loved ones surrounding you. You are receiving their kindness, love, and happiness. You are filled with kindness, love, and happiness.

- Silently and with sincerity, slowly and affectionately offer words of kindness and compassion to yourself, such as:

    - May I be safe and cared for

    - May I be happy

    - May I feel loved

    - May my heart and mind be awakened; may I feel free

    - May I accept myself as I am

    - May I live with ease

    - May I be peaceful

    - May I be free from pain

    - May I be kind to myself

    - May I accept myself as I am

- Now pause for a moment.

- If your mind wanders, return to the sensations in your body. Breathe naturally. Observe the gentle rise and fall of your chest. Repeat the loving-kindness phrases.

- Keep repeating the phrases silently, allowing yourself to feel any emotions that come up for you. You may feel anger, happiness, joy, sadness, or gratitude. Give yourself time to accept whatever feeling you have.

- Return to your heart center. Scan your body, relax, and feel comfortable.

- Shift your awareness to a person that you love and care about, or a loving pet. This should be someone kind and loving and who makes you smile and feel good. Visualize this person, and say his or her name. Now, quietly, and to yourself, offer them a compassionate phrase, such as "May you be happy and peaceful." Repeat this for 3-4 minutes.

- Complete the meditation by bringing your awareness back to yourself. Repeat a few loving kindness phrases to yourself.

- Taking a few deep breaths, and resting quietly in your body, enjoy the loving and kind feeling while keeping your eyes closed.

- Gently open your eyes.

SELF AFFIRMATIONS

Affirmations are statements you say to yourself with confidence. I used to visit a friend and find pink Post-It notes all over the place. They were everywhere. I went to see another friend, and she had statements written on her bathroom mirror. What was this? My friends were using mind tools, by writing affirmations in places where they would see them. They are positive beliefs and thoughts that are written into statements. They can be very useful tools to change your quality of life.

Affirmations can help you to visualize and believe in yourself, and to help encourage you to make positive changes in all aspects of your life. You can use these written statements as self-talk and in internal dialogues. They help you to challenge and overcome negative thinking and other self-sabotaging behaviors. Whether you realize it or not, your daily conversations are considered affirmations. We create and affirm life experiences with our thoughts and words. What you put out in the world is what comes back to you. If you say that you complain about what you don't want in your life, those complaints will keep on coming back. You need to affirm specifically what you want in your life. If you believe the affirmations that you are repeating, they are likely to actually happen. You need to observe your thoughts and eliminate the ones creating the experience that you don't want in your life. If you keep telling yourself that something will never happen, guess what? It WILL NOT HAPPEN.

Affirmations are a way to retrain our thinking, beliefs, and voices into positive paths that we would like to see happen in our lives. They involve consciously and carefully choosing words that

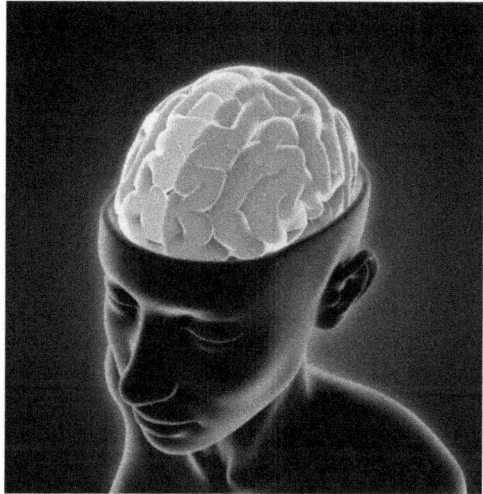

bring your life in a positive direction. This only works when you believe what your affirmation is saying. It is easy to produce positive statements: however, they can be just as easily over-ridden by the deep-rooted negative patterns in our unconscious mind. If you are just going through the exercise without intent and belief, it will be a wrap. No go.

Recite your chosen affirmations several times a day. I say mine in the morning and before I go to bed at night. And yes, I write them on my bathroom mirror and post them on my fridge.

If you feel negative thoughts coming and they are related to your affirmations, say your affirmation aloud. Choose affirmations that have a special meaning to you, to make it easier to feel them in your heart and soul when you say them. While I was writing this book, I repeated many times the affirmation "My book is finished, and I am moving!" I also affirmed that my heart was open.

Here are a few affirmations that you can start to use. It's useful to write your own as well. Notice that affirmations are always written in the present tense as if they are happening now. It strengthens your belief that the statement is true. You aren't saying that it was this way, or that it will be this way, but that it is this way NOW.

- I am wonderful, and I love myself
- I approve of and care for myself
- Self-compassion is an inside job: I am kind and gentle to myself
- I am human. I am not perfect, nor do I need to be perfect or want to be perfect.
- My confidence is soaring
- Every day I am growing, expanding, and thriving
- My happiness is my choice
- I am grateful for my great friends and my wonderful family
- People recognize my work, and I am admired
- My heart is open, and I know my love and partner is coming
- I am a powerhouse; I am indestructible
- Though these times are difficult, they are only a short phase in my life
- My efforts are being supported by the universe; my dreams manifest into reality before my eyes
- I radiate beauty, charm, and grace
- I am at peace with all that has happened, is happening, and will happen
- I am a spiritual and healing warrior
- My life is just beginning

- Empathy for others will open the doors for healing and compassionate connections inside and out
- I treat myself with care and compassion
- I can easily do this
- I radiate joy, love, and peace
- I am resilient
- Pain is out of my control, but self-compassion is in my control

CHAPTER ELEVEN

NEUROPLASTICITY: CHANGE YOUR BRAIN, CHANGE YOUR LIFE

Think not lightly of good, saying, "It will not come to me."
Drop by drop is the water pot filled.
Likewise, the wise one, gathering it little by little, fills oneself with good.
~ Dhammapada 9.122[20]

Let's start learning about neuroplasticity by describing how you start your day. How do you get into your mindset? What is the first thing that comes to your mind when the alarm goes off? Are they positive or negative thoughts? Are you sulking about your workload or the hassles of rounding up the troops and getting out of the house on time? Or do you take the time to notice the beauty of the sunrise and welcome the blessings of another day?

Are you tired of the negativity bias hijacking your brain? Do you no longer wish to recycle those negative memories and self-talk recordings? Some days were so stressful and disappointing for me before I even hit my foot to the floor. It was hard to muster the strength to even get out of bed in the morning Why bother? It was just Groundhog Day all over again. Nothing is good in my life, I thought. I felt stuck and overwhelmed in the chaos.

After maintaining a regular mindfulness practice and learning the benefits it had, I wanted to learn more. I began training in neuroplasticity.

---

20 The "Dhammapada" is a part of the "Pali Tipitaka," which is the sacred scripture of Theravada Buddhism.

I had the psychological background. Why not explore how to rewire my brain? It sounds very scientific and complicated. However, I am here to tell you that it works. I experienced it personally, and it has changed my whole mindset on life.

To enter this journey, you will need motivation and patience. It's like trying to fill a bucket of water one teaspoon at a time. It will take a while, but it can be done. It's worth the work. There are significant payoffs in having a resiliency in life and not constantly being pulled to the negative side. I have not completely turned off the sound of the negative self-talk recording completely, but my alarm goes off, and I am ready to switch to positivity. Rewiring your brain for the positive allows you to build up inner resources and inner strengths that are readily available to you when you are faced with daily challenges. It builds self-compassion. It sensitizes the brain for good. It gives your brain a positive bias to combat the powerful negativity bias. It also makes you want to spread your positivity and compassion more to others.

I might not be able to rewire a lamp with any kind of skill, but I have the control and skill set to rewire my brain. Here is how the process begins.

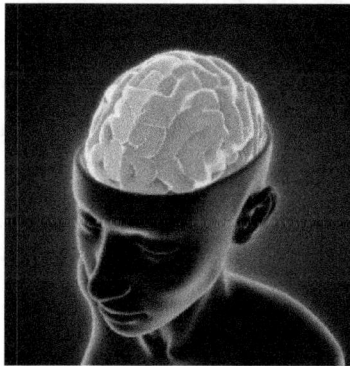

Your left prefrontal cortex (PFC) is associated with the more positive emotions. The more we can activate the left side of your PFC, the more your well-being is enhanced. The left PFC is responsible for controlling our negative emotions. You have to thoughtfully activate your left PFC in order to stop the negative thoughts and add the positive ones. If you just let the left PFC do its own thing, there will be no control over the negativity. So now you know that when you are with a constantly negative person, you can imagine their left PFC lighting up like a light bulb. Or, maybe, when you feel yourself in that negative mood, you can imagine that side of your brain turning red. A warning bell goes off. ALERT! ALERT!! A negative thought is coming...abort...abort...head to the positive!

Research shows that people who are under chronic stress release cortisol. Cortisol weakens the neurons in your hippocampus (seahorse.) This is the part of the brain that is responsible for your visual/spatial memory and your memory for context. As a result, deficits in this region due to a history of chronic stress will limit your ability to form new memories of the positive things you did today. Over time, it will also increase your sensitivity to stress. This leads to more stress. We become more stressed out and can't remember the fun things we did in any given day.

As your mind changes, your brain changes. These changes can be both short term and long term.

Let's say that every morning you have a gratitude practice. This will have temporary effects on your brain. As you list those things that you are grateful for, you will have temporarily affected the flow of reward-related neurotransmitters, like dopamine. This will brighten up your mind and increase the norephedrine. Personally, I need a shot of dopamine in the morning when I first wake up. So I replaced checking Facebook to see if I got any 'likes' to making a list of the things that I am grateful for. I get the bonus of brightening my mind.

What flows through your mind helps to sculpt your brain. As neuropsychologist Rick Hanson says, "Neurons that fire together wire together." As our minds are flowing, information from our brains to the central nervous system is sent. Based on the patterns etched by the flow of information, the repeated neural firing along the path of the signals through the central nervous system, changes in our neural structures can occur. The busy areas of the brain get more blood flow and start stitching other connections with each other's existing synapses. They become more sensitive and stronger. They build out more receptors. More receptors start new connections with each other, and new synapses are formed.

Research has also shown that people who have a regular meditative practice have thicker brains in the insula or the 'interception' areas. This is related to your ability to tune into your body and your deeper feelings. So, by staying in your present, practicing your breathing, and introspection, you can make permanent changes to your brain! It also strengthens your prefrontal cortex, which controls your ability to pay attention. By strengthening these areas, you can pay better attention to what your spouse or children are telling you. This will improve your familial relationships and decrease the number of misunderstandings that cause so much trouble.

It's impressive – and important – to know that we can lessen the chance of cortical thinning as we age if we just regularly meditate. Cortical thinning is serious business – it has been associated with depression and dementia and a whole host of other ills.

You can use your mind

To change your brain

To change your mind

For the BETTER!

So, what you focus your attention on during the day will help build lasting changes in your neural structures. It can cement the natural path for 'response mode' in your brain. If our focus is negativity, resentment, and complaining, the pathway heads directly to the left PFC. The opposite structure is built when we show gratitude, count our blessings, believe in ourselves, and celebrate our achievements, no matter how big or small they are.

Now that you know YOU have control of your brain, WHICH kind of path do you want your thoughts to flow down?

All of this sounds great, of course, but the ultimate question is this: if we CAN change our brains, why DON'T we?

Part of the problem involves our ability to hold our attention. With all of our multitasking and our external and internal distractions, we have developed really short attention spans and patience levels. All of these things compete for our attention and overwhelm our brains.

We can look around us and see nothing but negativity. I am well aware that there is no shortage of negative experiences around us on any given day. If you are hard pressed to find any, just turn on the local news. But I remind myself that my past negative experiences have also helped me to build my resiliency. Negativity lowers our mood, makes us anxious, and adds more stress, thus increasing our learned behaviors and skewing them towards negativity.

Knowing that the home base of our brains is that of calm, contentment and caring, you can deliberately change your mind for the better, despite all of the negative input. Just be aware that sometimes it will feel like you are swimming upstream. As you read this, your brain is scanning for negative news to overreact or over-focus on. Your brain, without your control, will install the negativity in your life so much faster than the positive.

Inner strengths are built from brain structures. We want to increase self-confidence, happiness, determination, and the feeling of being loved. So how do we get more of these in our brains? Positive qualities and strengths are built from positive experiences of strengths. For example, if you want more confidence, look for more active experiences in which you can get a sense of achievement.

The problem with getting these experiences into our brains is in the hardwire bias for negativity that we have. Negativity bias makes learning from bad experiences easier than learning from the good experiences. Good experiences seem to bounce off of our brains, and bad experiences naturally seem to sink it. It's like the childhood chant, only good experiences are the rubber, and bad experiences are the glue.

Think of it this way: if, during your annual review, your boss gave you five positive compliments, one negative criticism, and four neutral statements, which would you remember the most? Which statement would you turn over and over in your mind, festering like an infection in your brain? Which statement are you most likely to bring home with you? Yup, it's the one negative, even though it exists in a sea of positive and neutral. But only if we let it. According to Rick Hanson, "Hardwire Negative Bias causes a fundamental bottleneck in the brain that creates a weakness for our both formal and informal efforts to heal and grow and train ourselves in different ways. We are good at activating mental states, but not as good at installing them into our brains.[21]"

So then, how do we learn to take in the positivity and the good over the negativity and the bad? It's not as easy as hooking ourselves to a positive energy pump. It's a gradual process of opening up the negativity bias in the brain and slowly weaving the good and positive experiences in our lives and our brains. It takes time, motivation, and desire to change your life. One positive, mindful experience at a time.

Learn to Take in the Good

Turn positive events into positive experiences. All kinds of good things happen in our daily lives that we hardly notice. Usually, when someone turns to you and says something nice, you don't take a pause and take it in. What is your typical reaction when someone gives you a compliment? Do you feel good and soak it in? Or do you brush it off and keep going about your day? Do you take the time to thank the giver? If you do, is your "thanks" tossed off out of habit, or do you truly feel gratitude? Personally, I have a tough time receiving positive feedback or taking in a compliment.

---

21 "Hardwiring Happiness: The New Brain Science of Contentment, Calm, and Confidence." Kindle edition, by Rick Hanson, 2013 Harmony Books, NYC.

I have really worked on this. I feel uncomfortable. Now, I try to look at saying thank you as acknowledgment of the giver, which makes them feel good. It is also a signal to force myself to get out of my head. Accept the positive: install it in your brain. Don't want longer than five seconds to respond. If you don't respond within five seconds, the urge to respond at all will be lost. Use it quickly, or you just feed that negative claim in your head.

This is your chance to feel good about anything positive that happened today. No matter how big or small, there is *something* that happened today that is positive. Maybe someone gave you an unexpected compliment, you found a dollar on the ground, a person paid your coffee at Starbucks, you had an extra 10 minutes of sleep, or you had a snow day at home. Whatever gives you a temporary mindful tickle is good enough. I feel that every morning when I wake to a beautiful sunrise or when my two dogs look happy to see me awake. I feel the love!

HAVE A POSITIVE EXPERIENCE

Take 30 seconds to a minute more in this exercise. You can do it with your eyes opened or closed. (I prefer them closed.) Take a few deep breaths and exhale slowly. Relax. Get comfortable. Let go of any thoughts or emotions that are pestering you. Bring your attention to a pleasant sensation.

Take in a positive experience that is already there or create your own. Think of a person or an animal that you feel really loves and cares about you. It can be from your past or present. It's someone that makes you feel good and with whom you have had a warm and loving experience. It can be things or people you are grateful for, or accomplishments that made you feel proud.

You can also create a positive experience by looking for the good during an immediate situation or recent events. It could be a time when you stood up for yourself or times when you showed self-compassion. Feel what it's like to bring those emotions and attitudes to yourself.

Bring any of these positive events to the foreground of your awareness and let your attention shine a spotlight on it as long as it is positive. By bringing it to the foreground, you are not distracted by anything around you: you are just letting the event be. You are shifting your attention to something positive and beneficial. It's like when I find the most amazing pair of shoes. I am only focused on my thoughts of the shoe box opening. I am not distracted by the salespeople or other customers. I am staying focused and thinking of how happy I am being in my seat waiting to try them on. Nothing around me is distracting me. If my attention wanders, I gently bring it back. Only pick good, positive facts, attributes, or memories. Be kind to yourself.

- **Music.** Think of a song that brings you positive thoughts and feelings. Think of the whole experience, the sounds of the instruments, vocals, and the background noise. What personal memories are attached to the song? What emotions surface? What actions come to mind? Do you have the urge to dance?

- **Thoughts, ideas, beliefs, insights.** Think of positive previous conversations you've had with people you cared for and/or respected. For example, when I smell coffee, I think of my Dad and how I used to share my mornings with him as a child. I see him sitting in his chair at the table, sneaking me a sip of his coffee, and sending me off to school.

- **Emotions.** Try to remember feelings of gladness, gratitude, joy. Think about how those feelings lifted your mood and allow them to do so now. I love feeling happy and joyful: who doesn't? I have certain friends in my life that remind me of this. Take my friend Positively Pat. Just seeing a picture of her or a post on her Facebook page fills me with happiness.

- **Dreams**. Don't confuse this dreaming of what you don't have with a lack of fulfillment. These are your hopes, desires, wants and needs that make you happy. For example, I desire to stay strong, which builds my determination to do so and to make it happen, which makes me happy. I can explore that easily for 30 seconds. I also desire a white Tesla – this is an external desire and my goal for 2017. I have a smile on my face just thinking about the interior of the front seat.

- **Actions**. These are outward behaviors that make me happy. I picture myself at the batting cages, or hanging upside down in my yoga class. Sometimes I imagine myself being more assertive when someone is being too direct with me. Creating boundaries in a situation that calls for it is an action.

ENRICH AND EXPERIENCE

When you enrich and experience, you hold on to the experience, letting it grow and build in your mind. You feel it in your mind and try to sense it in your body. You allow yourself to fill up your mind with this one experience.

Enriching and experiencing is like eating a meatball and turning it into the most amazing piece of steak you have ever enjoyed. The taste, the smell, the whole experience feels like heaven. All of your senses become involved. When I wake up to an amazing sunrise, I take in the entire experience of the colors, the vibrancy, and how the colors change over time. I await for the next shift of change in the sky. I listen to the birds and their sounds, and how their reflections appear on the top of the water. I set my clock. Each morning, the skies are fresh and new, ready to tell me a novel story. I hold on to this experience as long as nature allows. It is breathtaking and never gets old.

Here is another example: I am taking a cooking class once a month with my best friend. Just taking in the new experience is joyful. I see all of the people; the food ready to be prepped; the sounds, smells, and tastes; the positive energy of the people happy to be there; the love in my heart to share the time with my friend; and the anticipation of the final product. It has so many of the elements I love: novelty, intensity, duration, salience, and multimodality.

"Great," I hear you thinking. "You have a great life and appreciate what you have. Why is this relevant to me?"

Try this:

- Hold on to your visualization for at least 20-30 seconds in a row. Pay attention to it for as long as you can. Your neurons are firing and rewiring! You are turning this into a lasting neural structure. Protect it. It will be a safe place that you can always return to.

- Grow it in your mind and your body and become more intense. What is it like? Enjoy it and make it last. Make it novel and new. (Go dopamine!) This will make a difference in your life.

- Recognize its personal relevance to you.

- Pay attention to the entire experience. Take in and examine the feelings, the smells, the sounds, tastes, and your thoughts. Allow the process to flow. Don't take charge of the process or try to control anything.

- Relax and treat this as a novel event; something new and fresh.

I think about a memory of a candy store in California. When you walk in, the smell hits you as soon as you enter. Even now, I can hear the "Welcome!" from the girl behind the counter. I smell fudge. I can feel the texture of the tasty morsel in my mouth. My mouth is watering as I remember this! I can feel the marble countertop, on which sits the free samples. I am aware of my desire to take as many pieces as I want. My desires are growing to sample other types of candies. I head right for the direction of the caramel apples. Yum! They are fresh, and the store sells 15 varieties. I envision the colors and textures of the apples, so beautifully displayed on the glass shelves. Which one should I choose? Should I bring it home whole or as them to slice it? Oh wait – she's offering me a sample of the apple of the day. I can taste the caramel and the tartness of the Granny Smith apple underneath it. I take my treat outside to eat it and enjoy the sunny California weather. This experience could last for long minutes if I allow it. I feel relaxed and joyful, and no matter what else is happening in my world at this moment, I am only taking in this memory and basking in the positivity. I am making room in my life – in my brain – for this good experience.

As I am building the intensity of my visit to the store, my levels of norepinephrine build as well. The more intensely I build this memory, the more I form new synapses, which are in turn getting hardwired into my brain. My dopamine levels rise as well, also promoting new synapses. All because I am mindfully remembering a pleasant experience. What's not to like about a candy apple? I made the experience positive and intense, and so I feel really good. To make it even better, I will have a lasting benefit due to the increased positive neural pathways I have wired into my brain. All from a simple visit to a candy store!

ABSORB IT

The first step was taking in the good – for me, thinking about the candy store. The second step was building up that sense memory and intensifying the sounds, smells, colors, and emotions of it by adding mental lighter fluid. Now it is time for step three: absorbing. It's experiencing how that apple tastes and how it feels entering my body. Or how I take in the sun's rays in the morning. The experience has landed!

After I experience the sunrise, I close my eyes and feel the joy flowing from the intense colors of blue and coral entering my heart and soul. I feel blissful. It's a positive kickoff to a positive day. I feel the gratitude of nature's beauty. I add this positive experience to my collection of inner resources to use when I am faced with greater challenges.

Think back to the times in your life when you said to yourself, "I will remember this moment forever!" Do you recall how it felt to absorb that special feeling in your heart and soul? Taking in the good helps us stay in the responsive mode versus the reactive mode. With this good, you are heightening the installation in your brain by intensifying and prolonging the neural activities in your brain and building neural structures.

Here's an exercise that will help you absorb the beauty and good around you:

- Sense this positive experience and specifically make an intention to have it sink into you and become a part of you. Feel the strength spreading into your body. Lean right into it. It's a shifting of your strength. I always picture a superhero putting on a cape or an outfit that gives her incredible strength. If you prefer, imagine the slow build up to a powerful shift.

- Picture the experience sinking into your body.

- Put this experience into your prime memory systems. Encode the experience into the neural structure.

- Try to visualize the intensity of this experience sinking into you like a bright light coming into and soothing you. Or, if you prefer, picture a sponge absorbing water from a bowl. You are already sensing the rewards: inner strength and inner freedom.

- Put this happy, joyful thought or memory in a resource chest that you build in your mind. This will allow you to take it with you wherever you go. You are on your own side and doing something for yourself. No one else will be as effective an advocate for you and take in the good like you can do yourself.

- Touch your heart if you like as you feel a sense of being cared about.

If you are using gratitude, do you actually feel a little more thankful after the experience? If so, were you able to let it sink in? I can feel the reward of my apple. I only bought one when I was celebrating something very special. So experiencing the sense memory brings me back not only to the pleasure of the apple itself but the celebrations.

LINK IT

We are faced with negative and unplanned challenges almost every day. This optional step in your brain-rewiring project is a little more complicated. I will try to simplify it as best I can. (Truly, I would encourage you to work with a trained professional to master this step.) You have to hold two experiences in your mind at the same time: the negative and the positive. Keep the positive experience prominently in your focus and awareness. Hold them for 10-30 seconds straight.

Don't allow yourself to be hijacked by the negative. If you do, you will gradually associate the whole experience with the negative. If the negativity grabs you, stop, and think only of the positive experience. If you feel up to it, try adding the negative experience again. If you don't, just stay with the positive experience.

Linking the positive with the negative will help you heal the pain of a negative experience by giving it a positive association.

When you are faced with a challenge or a negative situation, you can also do one of three things:

- Be with the negative. Look at it. Accept that it is what it is, no more and no less. Try to understand it.

- Let go of the negative. Release it when you can. Relax. Vent.

- Replace the negative with something positive by taking in the good.

When you have a positive experience, go ahead and have it! Enjoy it because it is right in front of you. It's not about covering the negative traits. Experience more good and see less bad. Take control of the negative bias. The good will act as a buffer to the impact of a situation that might make you become reactive.

One experience will not generally have a significant impact on your life. Rewiring your brain is a gradual process. Little by little, it adds up. It takes a lot of these positive experiences to make a significant change to your brain. It's best to establish a regular time to work on this process. Go ahead and put it on your calendar so you don't forget! I like to do it at night before I go to bed. I start off by activating a positive experience and thinking about my morning. I enrich it by thinking of the upcoming joy of the sunrise. I hold on to the experience as long as I can, feeling the intensity, the joy and peacefulness, and the senses in my body. I absorb the experience by visualizing the joy and bliss entering my body like a ray of sunshine. I can feel the warmth in my heart, and I smile because I feel happy.

Once I am immersed in this feeling, I link this warm, safe, and happy feeling with the feeling of how I felt earlier today when I dropped a cup of hot coffee in my lap. I was angry and embarrassed. I hold onto the positive and the negative experiences and link them together. I hold onto this dual feeling for 30 seconds. Then I try to do it again.

A regular routine will make a big difference. I have also been able to apply this to a deeper level. This involves examining my triggers and their sources as well as my responses to those triggers. This process also ends with linking. I was stunned with the results of this process. Not only was my negative bias noticeably decreasing, but I was able to really understand the sources of my triggers and how they sculpted my brain. It involved exploring my childhood and my negative experiences that have had a significant impact. Just identifying those triggers sets off an alarm for me to start linking the positive with the negative. For sure, I feel stronger, more centered, and more responsive. I have learned to lean more towards the positive side when faced with adversity.

Think of a relationship with someone that is rather contentious. Your interactions are not always the most positive, and there seems to be a great deal of tension. I am thinking of one of my nieces that I have spent very little time with. We have had precious few interactions over the years. Through the family grapevine, I heard that she is formulating opinions about me without any current or reliable information. She is making assumptions and judgments. To my face, she is always very nice. But when I turn away, not so much. A family event is upcoming: now is the time to find good in the bad and see the good in others, including my niece. I could be reactive and confront her. Or, I could choose to ignore her as if she did not exist. Or, I could be responsive. I can create good facts and have a good experience with my family. Following are some options I have:

I have a positive memory associated with my father's favorite tie tack. I carry it around. It makes me feel as if he were with me. I can take this tie tack with me to the family function. It will give me a boost and remind me to stay positive. I have to remember: dealing with my niece is not worth any drama in my life.

Or, I could activate a state of positive calm in my mind. I have trained myself to do this at will. This can activate neural circuits of positive states when I am stressed.

Another option is to create a positive experience at stressful family events by finding some good facts within whatever situation I am in. I can see this situation as an opportunity to find the good in the person and, if really stretched, I can always find good facts. For example, maybe my niece is wearing a beautiful outfit. Maybe her relationship with her brother is especially kind and loving. Maybe she has a wicked sense of humor. You can always find something if you look for it hard enough.

When faced with a challenging situation, take it in, self-activate positive experiences, enrich, absorb, and link the negative person with the positive traits that you have brought to your awareness through this process. There must be *something* positive you can bring to your awareness about this person. And just think: you have the power to make this into a positive, grow as a person, and at the same time rewire your brain!

If you had the very worst day at work and then your car battery died when you attempted to go home, seize the experience as a gain and a win. Sit in the car and take in the good for 20-30 seconds. Let it grow inside, intensify, and sink in. Maybe the weather is especially pretty, or you feel good in the outfit you are wearing. There are several kind strangers (or coworkers) who will help you jump your battery so you can get home. You may not like your job, but you are gainfully employed. Find *something* positive around you. Once you have done this, in the back of your mind, bring in the frustrations that you feel and link it with the positive feelings you have just stirred up. Feel the walls of self-caring wrap themselves around you. This warm, fuzzy feeling is so much better to focus on instead of your frustrating day. It's quiet in that car as you wait for assistance. Take it in, accept it, and find some joy.

Once you begin to practice with this at night or as a regular part of your routine, you can have the opportunity to go further into the process. We develop the neural structures of the responsive mood in terms of our needs for safety, satisfaction, and connection. We become harder to manipulate by the appeals of fear and anger so that we are able to increasingly meet the challenges and opportunities presented by the response mode. We can recover more quickly even when others, the world itself, or just parts of our mind are flashing a red warning light.

SIMPLE STEPS TO DEAL WITH EMOTIONAL UPSET

Let your mind rest on the good things in life. The bad things always naturally rest and stay longer. Shift when you feel stuck. Think of gains and wins. What happened that was good? Train your brain to start at the good, to see the upside of changes in life.

1. Realize that you are upset. It does not change the self-recording of negativity in your head, but it changes the experience you are having: you are watching the movie of your upset rather than being immersed in it.

2. Practice self-compassion. Think of examples of when you have shown compassion for a friend. When did you show yourself such compassion? You wouldn't let anyone say things to your friend that you are saying about yourself. So why do it? It's the sense of being cared about by your most intimate friend – yourself. You have skills and talents to draw upon. You have more resources within yourself than you give yourself credit for. Endurance is a strength. The ability to let go is a strength.

3. Get on your own side. Be an advocate for yourself. Be strong for yourself.

4. Devise a plan. Ask yourself: what am I going to do about this situation? What will I do differently in my head? I remind myself that the same circuits that helped our ancestors run away from charging lions are what cause this sensory response. It is my survival instinct that activates the parasympathetic nervous system.

5. Trust your gut. You know not everything you hear is true. Remember: our minds naturally focus more on the negative. Step back and trust your intuition. Our first thought or feeling is usually the right one. Don't force things to happen for the wrong reasons. How many times have you found the perfect dress, only to keep on looking and then return to the original dress after you've made five other choices?

6. Actively build up positive implicit memories to balance the unfair accumulation of negative memories. You already have a negative list prepared in your mind. I know it. If I asked you to write a list of 10 qualities, attributes, or physical features that you don't

like about yourself, it wouldn't take you but a few seconds. How long would it take you to write a positive list? Probably a whole lot longer. In order to train yourself to think positively, try the following:

7. Start a list of positive facts about yourself. Every day add something new that you discovered about yourself.

    - Write a list of positive experiences in your life, such as a birth of a child, your wedding, or your graduation.

    - Make a list of favorite vacations or a list of vacation spots on your bucket list. Be sure to say why they are on your list!

    - Make a list of your favorite friends, family members, and co-workers. These should be people who put a smile on your face.

    - Make a list of safe places. These are places you would go that make you feel safe and comfortable. I love my yummy bed. Or sitting outside on the dock. Sometimes just being alone gives me comfort, not matter where I am.

    - Compose a gratitude list of things in your life that you are thankful for.

When you are doing this, you are making a visual positive board in your mind of positivity. If it will help you, get an actual piece of poster board and make one using your lists, cut outs of pictures from magazines, and whatever else will make you happy. Surround yourself at work or at home with reminders of your mindful tickles. I do this every day when I look outside of my office and see the water. Or when my four-legged husband, Murphy, greets me with a sloppy kiss! I have a necklace that reminds me of happier times in my life. I feel happy when I wear it.

"Linking" is really more complicated than I described here. It involves exploring your triggers and noting when they occurred to see where you have stored it in your brain. Then, it is a daily process to link a positive with that triggered response and keep working on it until it is gone or less reactive. In other words, when something makes you mad at work, it isn't always the event itself that is causing such a reaction in your brain – it's something bigger and deeper in your past that is playing out.

The concept is that you create a beneficial experience, and you rewire your thought patterns to link the negative trigger with the positive experience. You can practice this with playing out scenarios in your head. The major benefit of this process is that it increases factors of mindfulness such as executive function, which in turn strengthens your PFC, and increases self-compassion, determination, and stress tolerance.

These processes help us grow inner resources that help us with anxiety, hurt feelings, addictions, and our need to assert ourselves. It heals old wounds, fills holes in your heart, and allows you to be active rather than passive. Negative experiences are pain with no gain. Wouldn't you rather treat yourself kindly by righting the negativity imbalance?

We are molding our minds to fit the positive experiences. If we don't actively do this, they will revert to the negative state. It is up to us to be the craftsman that shapes our own minds. This process disentangles us from the snarly feelings that cause unresolved cravings. We can increasingly rest peacefully, and spend our days in a state of contentment and love that has nothing to do with the external conditions around us.

Sometimes we block ourselves from taking in the good. Maybe we are too distracted, too uncomfortable to bring our attentions inward, or over-analytical. Sometimes people fear the disappointment of bringing things up. They feel like they are letting people off the hook by not assigning blame. Sometimes people feel like they do not deserve to feel better under the circumstances. None of this is true: it's all about identifying problematic beliefs, and finding and instilling new, true, and useful beliefs instead.

Your brain has a natural talent for learning from the bad experiences. You have to develop your talent to learn from good experiences. You can learn from tough times and gain from them. The world is tilted on its axis away from us, but if we are aware of this, we can rewire our neural pathways to anticipate the tilt and counterbalance it.

This process takes motivation and a whole lot of work, but it builds your brain and weakens the negativity bias. It's something that must be done at least five times a day to be effective. It only takes a few minutes – isn't it worth the time to turn the bad into good and really feel that change deep within your body?

CONCLUSION

"Very little is needed to make a happy life;
it is all within yourself, in your way of thinking."
~ Marcus Aurelius

It's hard for me to believe that this book is almost over. It has been a labor of love for over a year. If I had my druthers, I would keep on writing and never stop. Perhaps I'll continue the journey in another book.

As I set out to find the mind I thought I had lost, I needed to search for a direction that would lead me along the path towards my final journey. I needed to heal and thrive. Like so many people who face adversity, I felt invisible and broken to my core. I wanted to find my voice and independence. I wanted to synchronize my mind and body so that I could trust and love again.

If I have to be honest, I have to say that the process was filled with ups and downs. Initially, I was filled with uncertainty, fear, sadness, and vulnerability. I journaled all of my helpful mind tools. Meditation and mindfulness were my sanity and my protection. They provided me with clarity, inner peacefulness, and increased my trust in myself and my instincts. They gave me permission to give myself space to think before I spoke and be more thoughtful with my actions.

It was a process, learning to be alone so often. It was a contrast to the more hectic life I had in Miami. I quickly noticed that by being scared and wanting to escape my problems, I was missing out on my present and the beauty around me. It gave me an opportunity for introspection with an open mind. I examined my core values and beliefs, my past relationships, passions, and desires. I spent days without social media, television, or a telephone. After a brief withdrawal, I grew fond of being able to control my stimulation input. Silence was my key to listening to myself and trusting my instincts. I am lucky enough to have the gift of empathy. This healing time strengthened those skills as well.

Eventually, my lease on the sod farm ended. That year flew by! Spring and summer months came and went. I developed mind tools that helped me build a connection with my heart and soul. I found mental clarity and a psychological alignment. I took time for myself every day. I journaled what worked and what did not. I established a daily routine. I kept my promise to myself to set boundaries. I walked away from dysfunctional and negative relationships. I discovered new passions. I tried new ways to exercise. Some of them I loved, some challenged me, and some made me feel like I was going to die! I found my new love: aerial yoga. I kept my promise to spend the year focusing on my needs, building my core strengths, values, and inner resources. Most importantly, I found my voice, my power, and my story.

I learned that my gut instincts rarely fail me – so long as I listen to them.

I learned that I am strong. I do not need to fall into the same old trap and pattern, thinking that I need a man to pull me out of the wreckage. I can pull myself. I wake up every day and feel grateful. I list my things that I am grateful for, and say my self-affirmations before I even get out of bed. Then, the dogs jump on my bed, and I feel like the chips in a chocolate chip cookie. What love to feel every morning!

And then, I meditate.

I understand that gratitude brings joy, and joy brings abundance. It's such a feeling of love and peace. I am following my passion for helping people, something I have done my whole life. I have so many opportunities to look forward to this year. There are lectures, workshops, and a radio show. My heart is open. I am ready for my next chapter. I am whole and healed. I love and trust myself again. I have greater intuition and healing powers.

Suddenly, in September, I realized how much I loved living in this house I had leased and hated for so long. It had become MY house. Everything felt different.

The house felt brighter, warmer, and lighter. I enjoyed the outdoors, and all of the beautiful trees.

Through the mind tools I have described in this book, I have made a life for myself full of positivity, compassion, self-compassion, and happiness. Like any true convert, I want to share this joy with my friends, family, and anyone who is willing to hear it. I want you to find the self-trust, inner peace, and faith that I have found. That was the inspiration for this book. It is my passion to take my inner strength to create and use mind tools to help others live a happy and mindful life.

Go. Stay mindful, and be happy.

APPENDIX

MIND TOOL RESOURCES I USED THIS YEAR

Focus on what you choose – mental effectiveness. A focused mind does not multitask and is fully present on the person or task at hand. You recognize the overwhelming majority of distractions are irrelevant and can be put aside for the moment. This will increase your productivity and effectiveness.

Choose your distractions mindfully.

Learn in your life to take a short pause, focus on your breathing for a moment, and access the quality of your mind. This will increase your creativity, bolster resilience, sharpen your clarity, and improve your performance.

Set emotional and physical boundaries.

Are you making a choice or courting a woe?

Live as if you have the power to change the world. Remember – this day will never come again.

Don't fear big, then run away from big opportunities. Move past your doubts. It will help you experience your true potential in both work and life.

Don't have a mindset of fear of where life will take you. Failures are a part of our learning process. They keep us striving for our true potential.

Discover your purpose. Set your priorities, both long and short term goals. Write your goals in the following areas:

- Social/relationships
- Children
- Work
- Financial
- Spiritual
- Emotional
- Physical
- Intellectual

What is one thing you can do today to affirm your life's purpose? What is the one thing you can do for yourself today? Make time for yourself to seek clarity.

Practice being kind to yourself when you show love and compassion to yourself. Be aware of how you do or don't take care of yourself. Meditation is just one way.

Don't believe everything that you think. Get out of your own head.

Slow down. Monotask. Manage your attention and stay in your present.

Free yourself of fears, should, assumptions, and judgments.

Our bodies can change our minds, our minds can change our behaviors, and our behavior can change our outcomes. Check your posture. Find your POWER POSE!!! (If you can't think of one, start with the "Wonder Woman" pose – feet apart, shoulders back, chin up, hands on hips.) How powerful does it make you feel? Are you hunched over, closed up, and making yourself small? Or do you spread yourself wide open, arms out, and take space from around you? According to Social Psychologist Amy Cuddy, our nonverbal cues can often govern the way that we think about ourselves. Before you enter a stressful situation, STRIKE YOUR POSE. Take two minutes and expand yourself. Make a "V" with your body. Throw your arms into a V shape and reach upwards.

If you are sitting down, put both feet on the ground and give yourself lots of room. Sit with your chest open, shoulders back, chin up, and eyes level. Breathe slowly and deeply. At first, pretend to be powerful. Show it with your posture. Gradually, you will feel it inside and out. Your posture is a nudging way to remind yourself to be confident and reduce your cortisol. From time to time during the day, check your posture.

Find your purpose and your passions. Your path will reveal itself. This will increase your creativity, talents, and resiliency.

Establish your comfort zone, focus on your goals, aspirations, and don't stand in your own way. Write your goals.

Change it up! Create new neural pathways in your brain that create new habitual patterns. These newly rewired brain patterns can deepen your experiences and reinforce old behaviors (the positive ones!) that frame our self-identity.

Spend time alone with yourself. Don't attach yourself to who you think you should be. Consider who you are.

Rewire.

ABOUT THE AUTHOR

CYNTHIA L. DOUGHERTY, PH.D.

Cynthia has been in the "Helping" business for over two decades.

Her all-embracing wisdom comes from her training as a Wellness and Life Coach, a Certified Meditation Teacher, and a Certified School Psychologist. Cynthia also holds a Ph.D. in Human and Child Development, a Master's degree in Family Therapy and a Certificate in Neuropsychology.

Cynthia has practiced in a wide variety of settings including a clinical practice, schools, hospitals and major corporations. Cynthia now combines her psychology and therapy training with her love and passion and for neuroscience and mindfulness.

Cynthia believes that bringing mindfulness into your life both personally and in business will help you optimize your ability to create and live a happy, joyous and fulfilling life.

Awareness is the foundation of who we are and what we do and is the key to self-knowledge, transformation and being able to not just survive in the stressful world we live in, but to really thrive!

Cynthia helps people reduce their stress by teaching them how their brain operates and then showing them how to re-wire their brains using simple mind tools.

Cynthia enjoys coaching people in using mind tools to live a more fulfilling, happier and less fear-driven life.

You can reach Cynthia at her website: gratefulpeaceofmind.com

Thank you for reading!

I hope you enjoyed this book! I enjoyed writing it!

CAN YOU DO ME A FAVOR PLEASE -- It would help me spread the word to others if you could write a review of it on Amazon. Reviews help people who are deciding whether to purchase the book to make a decision. Reviews are not easy to get, so if you could take a few minutes to write one, I would be greatly obliged.

Just go to Amazon and write a review on my book page!

Remember, to pick up your FREE Gift, *10 Must-Have Mind Tools for Frazzled Women*, on my website at:

http://gratefulpeaceofmind.com/free-gifts/

BIBLIOGRAPHY

The Four Agreements: A Practical Guide to Personal Freedom (A Toltec Wisdom Book)
Nov 7, 1997
by Don Miguel Ruiz and Janet Mills

The Fifth Agreement: A Practical Guide to Self-Mastery (A Toltec Wisdom Book)
Jul 7, 2011
by Don Miguel Ruiz and Janet Mills

Soul-Centered: Transform Your Life in 8 Weeks with Meditation
May 1, 2012
by Sarah McLean

Simple, Easy, Every Day Meditation Method
Jul 6, 2013
by Sarah McLean

Best Seller
Hardwiring Happiness: The New Brain Science of Contentment, Calm, and Confidence
Oct 8, 2013
by Rick Hanson

Buddha's Brain: The Practical Neuroscience of Happiness, Love, and Wisdom
Nov 1, 2009
by Rick Hanson and Daniel J. Siegel

Mindful Work: How Meditation Is Changing Business from the Inside Out (Eamon Dolan)
Mar 10, 2015
by David Gelles

Resisting Happiness
Aug 15, 2016
by Matthew Kelly

The Happiness Equation: Want Nothing + Do Anything = Have Everything
Mar 8, 2016
by Neil Pasricha

The Art of Happiness, 10th Anniversary Edition: A Handbook for Living
Oct 1, 2009
by Dalai Lama

The Happiness Track: How to Apply the Science of Happiness to Accelerate Your Success
Jan 26, 2016
by Emma Seppala

The Selfish Brain: Learning from Addiction
Mar 16, 2000
by Robert L DuPont M.D.

Best Seller
Grit: The Power of Passion and Perseverance
May 3, 2016
by Angela Duckworth

Mindset: The New Psychology of Success
Feb 28, 2006
by Carol S. Dweck

Warren Buffett and the Interpretation of Financial Statements: The Search for the
Company with a Durable Competitive Advantage
Oct 14, 2008
Warren Buffett's Management Secrets: Proven Tools for Personal and Business Success
Dec 8, 2009
by Mary Buffett and David Clark

Emotional Habits: The 7 Things Resilient People Do Differently (And How They Can
Help You Succeed in Business and Life)
May 8, 2016
by Akash Karia

The Habit Project: 9 Steps to Build Habits that Stick (And Supercharge Your Productivity,
Health, Wealth and Happiness)
Aug 25, 2016
by Akash Karia

The Mindful Athlete: Secrets to Pure Performance
Apr 17, 2015
by George Mumford and Phil Jackson
The Champion's Mind: How Great Athletes Think, Train, and Thrive
May 15, 2015
by Jim Afremow

Relentless: From Good to Great to Unstoppable
Apr 16, 2013
by Tim S. Grover and Shari Wenk

Basketball Mindfulness 101: Learn to get in the zone, deliver in the clutch, and appreciate every moment on the court.
Nov 27, 2015
by Eric Duffett

The Four Noble Truths: The Foundation of Buddhist Thought, Volume 1
Jun 10, 2005
by Geshe Tashi Tsering and Gordon McDougall

Relative Truth, Ultimate Truth: The Foundation of Buddhist Thought, Volume 2
Oct 10, 2008
by Geshe Tashi Tsering and Gordon McDougall
Kindle Edition

Tantra: The Foundation of Buddhist Thought, Volume 6
Jul 10, 2012
by Geshe Tashi Tsering and Gordon McDougall

The 15 Commitments of Conscious Leadership: A New Paradigm for Sustainable Success
Jan 15, 2015
by Jim Dethmer and Diana Chapman

The 15 Commitments of Conscious Leadership: A New Paradigm for Sustainable Success
Jan 15, 2015
by Jim Dethmer and Diana Chapman

The Art of Mental Training - A Guide to Performance Excellence
Nov 5, 2013
by DC Gonzalez

Holographic Healing (5 Keys to Nervous System Consciousness Book 1)
Dec 19, 2012
by George Gonzalez
Kindle Edition

The Zen of Listening: Mindful Communication in the Age of Distraction
Dec 20, 2012
by Rebecca Z Shafir

Scarcity: Why Having Too Little Means So Much
Sep 3, 2013
by Sendhil Mullainathan and Eldar Shafir

The Five Keys to Mindful Communication: Using Deep Listening and Mindful Speech
to Strengthen Relationships, Heal Conflicts, and Accomplish Your Goals
Apr 10, 2012
by Susan Gillis Chapman

Shadow Work: The Unpaid, Unseen Jobs That Fill Your Day
May 1, 2015
by Craig Lambert

Clinical Neuroscience: Psychopathology and the Brain
Dec 7, 2010
by Kelly G. Lambert and Craig H. Kinsley

Clinical Neuroscience
Nov 26, 2004
by Kelly Lambert and Craig Howard Kinsley

Change Your Brain, Change Your Life (Revised and Expanded): The Breakthrough
Program for Conquering Anxiety, Depression, Obsessiveness, Lack of Focus, Anger, and
Memory Problems
Daniel G. Amen, M.D. Nov 3, 2015

Best Seller
The Brain Warrior's Way: Ignite Your Energy and Focus, Attack Illness and Aging,
Transform Pain into Purpose
Nov 22, 2016

Mindfulness at Work For Dummies
Apr 3, 2014
by Shamash Alidina and Juliet Adams

Mindfulness At Work Essentials For Dummies
Dec 9, 2014
by Shamash Alidina and Juliet Adams

Why Can't I Meditate?: How to Get Your Mindfulness Practice on Track
Apr 12, 2016
by Nigel Wellings

Transpersonal Psychotherapy

Jan 30, 2000
by Nigel Wellings and Elizabeth Wilde McCormick

Four Ways to Click: Rewire Your Brain for Stronger, More Rewarding Relationships
Feb 17, 2015 | Unabridged
by Amy Banks M.D. and Leigh Ann Hirschman

Wired for Dating: How Understanding Neurobiology and Attachment Style Can Help
You Find Your Ideal Mate Audible – Unabridged
Stan Tatkin PsyD MFT and Jonathan Yen

Your Brain on Love: The Neurobiology of Healthy Relationships Audible – Original
recording
Stan Tatkin (Author, Narrator), Sounds True (Publisher)

Positivity: Top-Notch Research Reveals the Upward Spiral That Will Change Your Life
Jan 27, 2009
by Barbara Fredrickson

Love 2.0: Finding Happiness and Health in Moments of Connection
Jan 24, 2013
by Barbara Fredrick

Flourish: A Visionary New Understanding of Happiness and Well-being
Apr 5, 2011
by Martin E. P. Seligma

Positivity: Groundbreaking Research Reveals How to Embrace the Hidden Strength of
Positive Emotions, Overcome Negativity, and Thrive
Jan 27, 2008
by Barbara Fredrickson

The How of Happiness: A New Approach to Getting the Life You Want
Dec 27, 2007
by Sonja Lyubomirsky

What You Can Change . . . and What You Can't*: The Complete Guide to Successful
Self-Improvement Kindle Edition
by Martin E.P. Seligman

Learned Optimism: How to Change Your Mind and Your Life, Kindle Edition
by Martin E.P. Seligman
Authentic Happiness: Using the New Positive Psychology to Realize Your Potential for
Lasting Fulfillment Kindle Edition
by Martin E. P. Seligman

Happiness at Work
Nov 18, 2013 | Kindle eBook
by Onno Hamburger and Ad Bergsma

Choke: What the Secrets of the Brain Reveal About Getting It Right When You Have To
Sep 21, 2010 | Kindle eBook
by Sian Beilock

One Second Ahead: Enhance Your Performance at Work with Mindfulness
Feb 16, 2016
by Hougaard, Carter and Coutts

How to Have a Good Day: Harness the Power of Behavioral Science to Transform Your Working Life
Feb 2, 2016 | Kindle eBook
by Caroline Webb

Powerful Poise: Secrets from Experts and Authors Amy Cuddy and Caroline Webb
Jul 30, 2016 | Kindle eBook
by Daniel Glick

Your Brain at Work: Strategies for Overcoming Distraction, Regaining Focus, and Working Smarter All Day Long
Oct 6, 2009 | Kindle eBook
by David Rock

Quiet Leadership: Six Steps to Transforming Performance at Work
Oct 13, 2009 | Kindle eBook
by David Rock

Coaching with the Brain in Mind: Foundations for Practice
Aug 6, 2009 | Kindle eBook
by David Rock and Linda J. Page

Quantum Healing (Revised and Updated): Exploring the Frontiers of Mind/Body Medicine
Nov 17, 2015
by Deepak Chopra

Reinventing the Body, Resurrecting the Soul: How to Create a New You
Oct 13, 2009
by Deepak Chopra

Creating Affluence: The A-to-Z Steps to a Richer Life
Jul 8, 2011
by Deepak Chopra and Richard Carlson

Perfect Health--Revised and Updated: The Complete Mind Body Guide
Dec 18, 2007
by Deepak Chopra M.D.

The Ultimate Happiness Prescription: 7 Keys to Joy and Enlightenment
Nov 17, 2009
by Deepak Chopra

The Heart of the Buddha's Teaching: Transforming Suffering into Peace, Joy, and Liberation
Jul 22, 2015
by Thich Nhat Hanh

Buddha's Brain: The Practical Neuroscience of Happiness, Love, and Wisdom
Nov 1, 2009
by Rick Hanson and Daniel J. Siegel

You Are Here: Discovering the Magic of the Present Moment
Dec 21, 2010
by Thich Nhat Hanh and Melvin McLeod

Teachings of the Buddha
Mar 13, 2012
by Jack Kornfield

Buddha: A Story of Enlightenment (Enlightenment Collection)
Oct 13, 2009
by Deepak Chopra

Radical Acceptance
Nov 23, 2004
by Tara Brach

True Refuge: Finding Peace and Freedom in Your Own Awakened Heart

Jan 22, 2013
by Tara Brach
Kindle Edition

The Gifts of Imperfection: Let Go of Who You Think You're Supposed to Be and Embrace Who You Are

Sep 20, 2010
by Brene Brown

The Wise Heart: A Guide to the Universal Teachings of Buddhist Psychology
Apr 29, 2008
by Jack Kornfield

The Art of Forgiveness, Lovingkindness, and Peace
Nov 26, 2008
by Jack Kornfield

After the Ecstasy, the Laundry: How the Heart Grows Wise on the Spiritual Path
Oct 2, 2001
by Jack Kornfield

A Lamp in the Darkness: Illuminating the Path Through Difficult Times
Mar 1, 2014
by Jack Kornfield and Jon Kabat-Zinn

Meditation for Beginners
Aug 1, 2008
by Jack Kornfield

Anatomy of the Spirit: The Seven Stages of Power and Healing
Sep 4, 2013
by Caroline Myss

Sacred Contracts: Awakening Your Divine Potential
Sep 4, 2013
by Caroline Myss

Entering the Castle: An Inner Path to God and Your Soul
Mar 6, 2007
by Caroline Myss

Why People Don't Heal and How They Can
Sep 4, 2013
by Caroline Myss

The Creation of Health: The Emotional, Psychological, and Spiritual Responses That Promote Health and Healing: Three Rivers...
Sep 23, 2009
by Caroline Myss and C. Norman Shealy Md

Loving What Is: Four Questions That Can Change Your Life

May 7, 2002
by Byron Katie and Stephen Mitchell
A Thousand Names for Joy: Living in Harmony with the Way Things Are
Feb 6, 2007
by Byron Katie and Stephen Mitchell

The Four Questions: For Henny Penny and Anybody with Stressful Thoughts
Jul 12, 2016
by Byron Katie and Hans Wilhelm

Mindfulness for Beginners: Reclaiming the Present Moment—and Your Life
Jan 1, 2012
by Jon Kabat-Zinn
Bestseller

The Miracle of Mindfulness: An Introduction to the Practice of Meditation
Apr 5, 1996
by Thich Nhat Hanh and Vo-Dihn Mai
Kindle Edition

From Stress to Stillness: Tools for Inner Peace
Nov 18, 2013
by Gina Lake
The Mindful Way through Depression: Freeing Yourself from Chronic Unhappiness
Feb 8, 2012
by Mark Williams

Wherever You Go, There You Are: Mindfulness Meditation In Everyday Life
Jul 1, 2009
by Jon Kabat-Zinn
Kindle Edition

Authentic Happiness: Using the New Positive Psychology to Realize Your Potential for
Lasting Fulfillment
Oct 2, 2002
by Martin E. P. Seligman

Alex M. Wood et al., "The Role of Gratitude in the Development of Social Support,
Stress, and Depression: Two Longitudinal Studies," Journal of Research in Personality
42, no. 4 (2008): 854– 71, DOI: 10.1016/ j.jrp. 2007.11.003. 36.

The Happiness Track: How to Apply the Science of Happiness to Accelerate Your Success
(p. 192).
Seppala, Emma (2016-01-26). HarperCollins, Kindle Edition.

Grit: The Power of Passion and Perseverance
Duckworth, Angela (2016-05-03). e (p. 285). Scribner. Kindle Edition.

"I was tired, lonely, frustrated": Michael D. Matthews, Head Strong: How Psychology Is Revolutionizing War (New York: Oxford University Press, 2014), 16.

G. Rein, M. Atkinson and R. McCraty. (1995), "The Physiological and Psychological Effects of Compassion and Anger," Journal of Advancement in Medicine, Vol. 8, No. 2: 87– 105. 3. C. Peterson, N. Park and M. E. P. Seligman et al. (2005), "Orientations to Happiness and Life Satisfaction: The Full Life vs. the Empty Life," Journal of Happiness Studies, Vol. 6: 25– 41. Strategy

One Second Ahead: Enhance Your Performance at Work with Mindfulness (pp. 222-224). Hougaard, Rasmus; Carter, Jacqueline; Coutts, Gillian (2015-11-03). Palgrave Macmillan. Kindle Edition.

D. Lohmar (2006), "Mirror Neurons and the Phenomenology of Intersubjectivity," Phenomenology and the Cognitive Sciences, Vol. 5, No. 1: 5– 16.

The Storyteller's Secret: From TED Speakers to Business Legends, Why Some Ideas Catch On and Others Don't
Feb 23, 2016 by Carmine Gallo Kindle Edition

The Mindful Leader: Awakening Your Natural Management Skills Through Mindfulness Meditation
Dec 16, 2008
by Michael Carroll

Inside The Yoga Sutras: A Comprehensive Sourcebook for the Study and Practice of Patanjali's Yoga Sutras
Jun 22, 2012
by Jaganath Carrera

The Yoga Sutras of Patanjali—Integral Yoga Pocket Edition: Translation and Commentary by Sri Swami Satchidananda
Jun 17, 2015
by Swami Satchidananda

The Places That Scare You: A Guide to Fearlessness in Difficult Times (Shambhala Classics)
Aug 13, 2002
by Pema Chodron

Pema Chödrön's Compassion Cards: Teachings for Awakening the Heart in Everyday Life

Nov 15, 2016
by Pema Chodron

Fearless at Work: Timeless Teachings for Awakening Confidence, Resilience, and Creativity in the F ace of Life's Demands
Nov 13, 2012
by Michael Carroll

Living Beautifully: with Uncertainty and Change
Oct 9, 2012
by Pema Chodron

When Things Fall Apart: Heart Advice for Difficult Times (Shambhala Classics)
Sep 26, 2000
by Pema Chodr

The Wisdom of No Escape: And the Path of Loving Kindness
Aug 21, 2001
by Pema Chodron

Awake at Work: 35 Practical Buddhist Principles for Discovering Clarity and Balance in the Midst of Work's Chaos
Paperback – February 14, 2006
by Michael Carroll (Author)

The Diamond Cutter: The Buddha on Managing Your Business and Your Life
Sep 1, 2009
by Geshe Michael Roach and Lama Christie McNally

The Essential Yoga Sutra: Ancient Wisdom for Your Yoga
Feb 4, 2009
by Geshe Michael Roach and Lama Christie McNally
Kindle Edition

Karmic Management: What Goes Around Comes Around in Your Business and Your Life
Sep 1, 2009
by Geshe Michael Roach and Lama Christie McNally

The Book
Sep 29, 2011
by Geshe Michael Roach
Discover Your True North
Aug 10, 2015
by Bill George and David Gergen

The Discover Your True North Fieldbook: A Personal Guide to Finding Your Authentic Leadership (J-B Warren Bennis Series)
Jul 15, 2015
by Nick Craig and Bill George

Authentic Leadership: Rediscovering the Secrets to Creating Lasting Value
Aug 1, 2003
by Bill George

Mind: A Journey to the Heart of Being Human
Oct 18, 2016
by Daniel J. Siegel M.D.

The ONE Thing: The Surprisingly Simple Truth Behind Extraordinary Results
Apr 1, 2013
by Gary Keller and Jay Papasan

The Whole-Brain Child: 12 Revolutionary Strategies to Nurture Your Child's Developing Mind
Oct 4, 2011
by Daniel J. Siegel and Tina Payne Bryson

Mindsight: The New Science of Personal Transformation
Jan 12, 2010
by Daniel J. Siegel

No-Drama Discipline: The Whole-Brain Way to Calm the Chaos and Nurture Your Child's Developing Mind
Sep 23, 2014
by Daniel J. Siegel and Tina Payne Bryson

The Developing Mind, Second Edition: How Relationships and the Brain Interact to Shape Who We Are
Feb 4, 2015
by Daniel J. Siegel M.D.

The Mindful Brain: Reflection and Attunement in the Cultivation of Well-Being (Norton Series on Interpersonal Neurobiology)
Apr 17, 2007
by Daniel J. Siegel

Finding the Space to Lead: A Practical Guide to Mindful Leadership
Sep 29, 2015
by Janice Marturano

Happiness: A Guide to Developing Life's Most Important Skill
Dec 14, 2008
by Matthieu Ricard and Daniel Goleman

Altruism: The Power of Compassion to Change Yourself and the World
Jun 2, 2015
by Matthieu Ricard

Why Meditate?: Working with Thoughts and Emotions
Sep 1, 2010
by Matthieu Ricard

Art of Meditation
Sep 1, 2011
by Matthieu Ricard

The Relaxation Response
Sep 22, 2009
by Herbert Benson M.D. and Miriam Z. Klipper

Relaxation Revolution: The Science and Genetics of Mind Body Healing
Jun 22, 2010
by Herbert Benson and William Proctor

Timeless Healing: The Power and Biology of Belief
Jul 7, 2009
by Herbert Benson

Thanks! How the New Science of Gratitude Can Make You Happier
Aug 6, 2007
by Robert Emmons

Gratitude Works! A 21-Day Program for Creating Emotional Prosperity
Apr 1, 2013
by Robert A. Emmons

Thanks! How Practicing Gratitude Can Make You Happier
Nov 6, 2008
by Robert Emmons

Turfgrass Science and Management
Jan 14, 2015
by Robert Emmons and Ph.D. Frank Rossi
Hardcover

Anxious: Using the Brain to Understand and Treat Fear and Anxiety
Jul 14, 2015
by Joseph LeDoux

The Emotional Brain: The Mysterious Underpinnings of Emotional Life
Sep 22, 2015
by Joseph Ledoux

Synaptic Self: How Our Brains Become Who We Are
Jan 28, 2003
by Joseph LeDoux

Memory Reconsolidation: Chapter four. Reconsolidation of Pavlovian Conditioned Defense Responses in the Amygdala
Mar 18, 2013
by Jacek Dębiec and Joseph E. LeDoux

The Upside of Stress: Why Stress Is Good for You, and How to Get Good at It
May 5, 2015
by Kelly McGonigal

The Willpower Instinct: How Self-Control Works, Why It Matters, and What You Can Do to Get More of It
Dec 29, 2011
by Kelly McGonigal Ph.D.

Summary of 'The Willpower Instinct' by Kelly McGonigal Ph.D. (2 Summaries in 1: In-Depth Summary and Bonus 2-Page PDF.)
Jun 5, 2015
by edify.me

Mindfulness, Bliss, and Beyond: A Meditator's Handbook
Aug 10, 2006
by Brahm and Jack Kornfield

The Art of Disappearing: Buddha's Path to Lasting Joy
Oct 20, 2011
by Brahm

Why Zebras Don't Get Ulcers: The Acclaimed Guide to Stress, Stress-Related Diseases, and Coping - Now Revised and Updated
Sep 15, 2004
by Robert M. Sapolsky

The Great Courses: Biology and Human Behavior: The Neurological Origins of Individuality
2005
by Robert Sapolsky

Neuroscience: Exploring the Brain
Feb 3, 2015
by Mark F. Bear and Barry W. Connors

Principles of Neural Science, Fifth Edition (Principles of Neural Science (Kandel))
Oct 26, 2012
by Eric R. Kandel and James H. Schwartz

Neuroscience For Dummies
Nov 28, 2011
by Frank Amthor

What Makes Your Brain Tick? Strategies for Improving Brain Function and Memory
Dec 7, 2016
by Crystal Oakley

ACKNOWLEDGEMENTS

With an open heart, I want to express my deepest and most loving gratitude to all of those who have inspired, supported, loved and supplied wisdom and patience over this past year. This journey included a great deal of seclusion and retreat, which limited my connection with so many family and friends. For those of you who respected and understood my need for detachment without judgment or guilt, I cannot thank you enough. Thank you, Dawn Lednum for finding me the perfect setting on Abundance Lane. I moved in with resistance and am moving out healed and determined.

I am especially grateful for my children Morgan and Shelby whom I love deeply. I honor our deep affection and connection. Don't let fear be your guide. Instead, take a leap of faith, be bold and stay in your present. Friends and family provided me love and support when writing this book. I have experienced many challenges in life, and I am blessed to have the love of my mother Ruth and my sister Colleen. Your support and joy has kept me going. And, of course, Gail! She is an inspiration to all of us. She taught me how to be kind and love unconditionally. I am so blessed to have such amazing friends that are my little treasures. I am beyond grateful for your messages of encouragement and continued messages to "get it done." You are all in my heart forever, Judi Amick and Becki, George and Pam, The St. Mike's gang, Gina and Charles, Dawn and Mimi. To Kathy and Glen Fong, who shared my mindfulness and spirituality, I am appreciative more than my words can convey. I could not have started this book without you. To a wonderful group of friends who are also authors and know first-hand of the growing pains of giving birth to a book, Cindy Papale-Hammontree, "Miami Breast Cancer Experts." Cindy, you gave me the courage to own my passion and to not look back! And soul sister

Patricia San Pedro, "The Cancer Dancer," "Dish and Tell," Pat, you are such a role model, healer, and True Friend. I adore you and thanks for believing in me and for supporting me mentally. We have so much more work to do, the possibilities are endless! You are so pure and blessed. Such an honor to have your help with this book. Your very presence touches my soul.

My soul twin Vanessa Holloway, such love and gratitude. You have taught me to use my gifts without fear or hesitation. And Amanda Freed, my best Yogi friend and sister. Thank you for hiding me in Tucson this summer and all of your Spiritual wisdom. I can't express enough gratitude to Sarah McLean. You saved my life and taught me well. Sarah, you have been an inspiration to so many people. You are a pure soul with a heart of gold. To all of my dear friends and study buddies at the McLean Meditation Institute. Especially, Peggy and Christina. We built a spiritual connection and bond that will last forever.

To Bunny, thank you for your kindness, seeing me like no other, for having such a loving heart. Our friendship is a gift that is precious. You have such strength and are my hero! To Dr. Henry Soper, dear friend and mentor. You opened my world to Neuropsychology! Your knowledge of the brain is over the moon! You are a gifted and talented man. My chief of mental health support and always available when I need a friend. You are a family member to me and the kids.

I could not have written this book without the help of Daria Anne DiGiovanni and Lisa Tarves from Writestream Publishing. Your help was truly a gift. To Michelle Kulp, I offer my gratitude and my friendship. I honor your intentions and guidance through this writing experience. Your book launches are pure genius. Your passion for books is a blessing and needs to be shown to the world. To my amazing editor, Lori Brudner Duff you gave me the wind beneath my wings to finish this book. You saw my journey so clearly and effortlessly. I could not ask for more as a partner in crime. We too have so much more collaborating to do, and souls to touch.

To Jennifer Loppolo. I sat in a temple and prayed for you to come to my life and a week later you entered. I needed someone to hear my voice and purpose. You listened and created my vision. So, blessed and grateful. This is such a beginning for us. I stayed in my land, and the universe brought me what I needed.

With an open heart and gratitude, I would like to thank all of those who have inspired me and supported me during my life's journey. I would not be the person that I am today without you being in my life. To Murphy the best four-legged love of my life. To my Father, who taught me to do what you love and follow your passion! Finally, I would like to say thank you to my readers. I hope this book inspires and motivates you to try some of the Mind Tools offered. Just giving your brain a 10-minute break through meditation can be life changing. Peace and Out!

NOTES

www.ingramcontent.com/pod-product-compliance
Lightning Source LLC
LaVergne TN
LVHW051509080426
835509LV00017B/1994